Supporting Windows 8

Featuring the Latest Windows 8.1 Release

Addendum to A+ Guide to Managing and Maintaining Your PC, Eighth Edition, and A+ Guide to Software, Sixth Edition

Jean Andrews, Ph.D.
Joy Dark

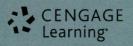

CENGAGE Learning®

Australia • Brazil • Japan • Korea • Mexico • Singapore • Spain • United Kingdom • United States

CENGAGE Learning®

Supporting Windows 8: Featuring the Latest Windows 8.1 Release
Jean Andrews

Vice President, General Manager: Dawn Gerrain

Product Director: Kathleen McMahon

Product Team Manager: Nick Lombardi

Director, Development: Marah Bellegarde

Product Development Manager: Leigh Hefferon

Senior Content Developer: Michelle Ruelos Cannistraci

Developmental Editor: Deb Kaufmann

Product Assistant: Scott Finger

Market Development Managers: Eric La Scola

Marketing Manager: Scott Chrysler

Production Director: Andrew Crouth

Content Project Manager: Allyson Bozeth

Manufacturing Planner: Ron Montgomery

Rights Acquisition Specialist: Alexandra Ricciardi

Production Service: Integra

Cover Designer: GEX Publishing Services

Cover Image: ©Shutter_M/Shutterstock

For product information and technology assistance, contact us at
Cengage Learning Customer & Sales Support, 1-800-354-9706
For permission to use material from this text or product,
submit all requests online at **www.cengage.com/permissions.**
Further permissions questions can be e-mailed to
permissionrequest@cengage.com

Library of Congress Control Number: 2013953070

ISBN-13: 978-1-285-84306-3

Cengage Learning
200 First Stamford Place, 4th Floor
Stamford, CT 06902
USA

Cengage Learning is a leading provider of customized learning solutions with office locations around the globe, including Singapore, the United Kingdom, Australia, Mexico, Brazil, and Japan. Locate your local office at: **www.cengage.com/global**

Cengage Learning products are represented in Canada by Nelson Education, Ltd.

To learn more about Cengage Learning, visit **www.cengage.com**

Purchase any of our products at your local college store or at our preferred online store **www.cengagebrain.com**

Notice to the Reader

Printed in the United States of America
1 2 3 4 5 6 7 18 17 16 15 14

Brief Contents

Table of Contents

Introduction

Supporting Windows 8 contains three new chapters about Microsoft's latest desktop operating system, Windows 8, featuring the Windows 8.1 release. It is meant to accompany *A+ Guide to Managing and Maintaining Your PC, 8ᵗʰ Edition*, and *A+ Guide to Software, 6ᵗʰ Edition*. It builds on the material in these core books and provides an in-depth look at using, installing, maintaining, securing, and troubleshooting Windows 8. An abundance of screenshots and step-by-step instructions guide students through the process of learning to support this new OS. Labs to accompany each chapter are found in the back of the book.

For more information about *A+ Guide to Managing and Maintaining Your PC* or *A+ Guide to Software*, please contact your sales representative or go to *www.cengage.com*.

FEATURES

To make the book function well for the individual reader as well as in the classroom, you'll find these features:

- ▲ **Learning Objectives:** Every chapter opens with a list of Learning Objectives that sets the stage for the goals and content of the chapter.
- ▲ **Step-by-Step Instructions:** Detailed information on installation, maintenance, optimization of system performance, and troubleshooting are included throughout the book.
- ▲ **End-of-Chapter Material:** Each chapter closes with the following features, which reinforce the material covered in the chapter and provide real-world, hands-on testing of the chapter's skill set:

  - **Chapter Summary:** This bulleted list of concise statements summarizes all the major points of the chapter.

  - **Key Terms:** The new, important terms introduced in the chapter are defined at the end of the chapter.

  - **Reviewing the Basics:** A comprehensive set of review questions at the end of each chapter checks your understanding of fundamental concepts.

  - **Thinking Critically:** This section presents you with scenarios that require you to use both real-world common sense and the concepts you've learned in the chapter to solve problems or answer questions.

  - **Hands-On Projects:** Several in-depth, hands-on projects are included at the end of each chapter; they are designed to ensure that you not only understand the material, but also can apply what you've learned.

  - **Real Problems, Real Solutions:** These projects give you valuable practice in applying the knowledge you've gained in the chapter to real-world situations, often using your own computer or one belonging to someone you know.

▲ **Figures:** Where appropriate, photographs of hardware and screenshots of software are provided to increase student mastery of the topic.

▲ **Notes:** Note icons highlight additional helpful information related to the subject being discussed.

▲ **To Learn More:** Where information in this book builds on concepts and skills covered in the main textbooks, references lead you to pages in those books where you can review this related content.

▲ **Website:** For additional content and updates to this book and information about our complete line of CompTIA A+ and PC Repair topics, please visit our website at *www.cengage.com/pcrepair*.

INSTRUCTOR RESOURCES

Answers to all end-of-chapter material, including Review Questions and Critical Thinking questions, and answers to Review Questions in the labs at the end of the book are provided to instructors online at the textbook's website.

Please visit *login.cengage.com*, and log in to access instructor-specific resources.

To access additional course materials, please visit *www.cengagebrain.com*. At the *CengageBrain.com* home page, search for the ISBN of your title (from the back cover of your book) using the search box at the top of the page. This will take you to the product page where these resources can be found.

ACKNOWLEDGMENTS

When Microsoft releases a new operating system, we here at Cengage Learning begin to respond in many ways. Part of that response is making sure that instructors and students have all the materials they need to successfully include the new OS in their curriculum. This book should do just that. The following reviewers all provided invaluable insights and showed a genuine interest in the book's success: Thank you to Melissa Bryant, Forsyth Technical College and June West, Spartanburg Community College. Thank you to Deb Kaufmann, the development editor, for your careful attention to details. It has been a pleasure working with you.

The labs at the end of the book were written with the exceptional help of awesome collaborators. We're grateful for the help of Gerald Kearns, Forsyth Technical Community College, and June West.

This book is dedicated to the covenant of God with man on earth.

— Jean Andrews, Ph.D.

— Joy Dark

WANT TO CONTACT THE AUTHOR?

Jean's expertise in PC Repair and A+ Certification has been a resource for instructors and students alike for years. If you'd like to give any feedback about the book or suggest what might be included in future books, please feel free to e-mail Jean Andrews at jeanandrews@mindspring.com or Joy Dark at joydark@mindspring.com.

Using Windows 8

Windows 8, 7, Vista, and XP all share the same basic architecture, and Microsoft has announced that Windows 9, expected to be out in 2014, will also use this same architecture. As a computer support technician, it's comforting to know that under the hood all these operating systems are similar, and the OSs have some common utilities, tools, and techniques used for troubleshooting. Windows 8 is the most stable OS Microsoft has produced to date, and supporting a Windows OS is actually getting easier even though the OS is getting more complex and offers many new features.

It's clear that Microsoft designed Windows 8 with the needs of the end user driving the design. Although the architecture might be similar, the user experience of Windows 8 varies greatly from the user experience of Windows 7. In this chapter, you'll first look at the interfaces offered to the user and explore the basics of using Windows 8.

> **? To Learn More** This book about Windows 8 is intended to be used as a supplement to accompany *A+ Guide to Managing and Maintaining Your PC, 8th Edition*, or *A+ Guide to Software, 6th Edition*. These two core textbooks contain many concepts and explanations about the Windows 7 operating system and how to support it that also apply to Windows 8. See one of these two core books for further explanations and concepts not covered in this book on Windows 8. In this book, we assume you're already familiar with Windows 7 and know how to support it.

> **Notes** Labs to accompany this chapter can be found in Lab A near the back of this book.

> **Notes** This chapter is written to follow Chapter 3 in *A+ Guide to Managing and Maintaining Your PC, 8th Edition*, or Chapter 1 in *A+ Guide to Software, 6th Edition*.

WHAT'S NEW WITH WINDOWS 8

Before you get started learning to use Windows 8, let's take a quick look at the new features you'll find when you use and support it.

> **Notes** This chapter assumes Windows 8 is already installed on your computer. If Windows 8 is not yet installed, read Chapter 2 and install Windows 8. Then you can return to this chapter to learn how to use the OS.

The editions of Windows 8 include Windows 8, Windows 8 Professional, Windows 8 Enterprise, and Windows RT. Here's a brief list of new features of all editions that apply mainly to the end user:

▲ *The Start screen:* The most obvious new feature is the Start screen that's especially designed for mobile devices, touch screens, lean apps that use few system resources, social media, social networking, and the novice end user (see Figure 1-1). The **Start screen** is used instead of the Start button on the Windows desktop to start an app, and apps on the Start screen appear as tiles. Click a tile to open its app. Some apps use **live tiles**, which offer continuous real-time updates. For example, the People app has a live tile to make it easy to keep up with updates on Facebook, LinkedIn, and Twitter.

> **Notes** The figures and steps in this book use Windows 8.1 Professional. If you are using a different edition of Windows 8, your screens and steps may differ slightly from those presented here.

Figure 1-1   The Windows 8 Start screen is used to view app tiles and to open apps
Used with permission from Microsoft Corporation

> **Notes** To conserve system resources, you can turn off a live tile. To do so, right-click the tile on the Start screen and then click **Turn live tile off** in the status bar that appears at the bottom of the screen. You can also use Task Manager to find out how the app is affecting overall system performance.

1

▲ *The Windows 8 interface:* Windows 8 has two interfaces: The new Windows 8 interface, also called the modern interface (shown in Figure 1-1), and the traditional Windows desktop. The **Windows 8 interface** uses pages rather than the windows used on the desktop. The interface is specifically designed for touch screens and for social and gaming apps. Productivity software, such as Microsoft Office, QuickBooks, and Dreamweaver, still use the Windows desktop (see Figure 1-2).

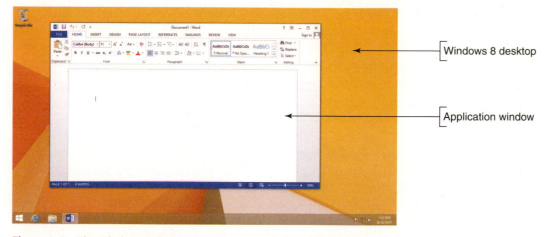

Windows 8 desktop

Application window

Figure 1-2 The Windows 8 desktop manages apps designed for this interface; use the Windows key to toggle between the Start screen and the desktop
Used with permission from Microsoft Corporation

▲ *SkyDrive:* When you use a valid email address to set up a **Microsoft account** at live.com, you get 7 GB of free cloud storage called a **SkyDrive**. Windows 8 is designed to fully integrate with your SkyDrive so you can easily store your data in the cloud. When you open the SkyDrive app on the Start screen, you see the folders at the root level of your SkyDrive (see Figure 1-3). Right-click white space on the page to see the status bar where you can create new folders. Click a folder to see its contents, and right-click a folder or file to see options to manage the item, such as delete, copy, cut, or rename a folder or file or add files to a folder.

▲ *Windows Store:* Apps that use the Windows 8 interface are purchased and downloaded from the **Windows Store** in a similar way that apps on smart phones and tablets are purchased. You cannot legally install an app in the Windows 8 interface

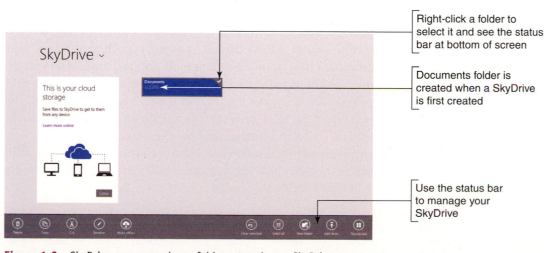

Right-click a folder to select it and see the status bar at bottom of screen

Documents folder is created when a SkyDrive is first created

Use the status bar to manage your SkyDrive

Figure 1-3 SkyDrive app page shows folders stored on a SkyDrive
Used with permission from Microsoft Corporation

without going through the Windows Store. (Illegally installing apps without using the Windows Store is called sideloading.) Also, you must have a Microsoft account to get apps from the Windows Store, even the free ones.

▲ *Microsoft account:* Besides signing into Windows using a local account or domain account, you can also sign in using your Microsoft account, which is linked to an email address and password. When you do that, you are automatically signed into your SkyDrive and other online accounts tied to your Microsoft account. When you sign in with a Microsoft account, your Windows 8 personalized settings and apps are stored at live.com and can be synced with up to five Windows 8 computers that you use.

▲ *File History:* File History is an easy-to-use tool for backing up personal data stored on the hard drive.

For the support technician and system administrator, Windows 8 is an extremely stable OS with several new technical features including:

▲ *Windows 8 ARM support:* The ARM processor and chipset hardware architecture is used on many smart phones, tablets, and other mobile devices, and the mobile edition of Windows 8, called Windows RT, supports this platform.

▲ *Storage Spaces:* Storage Spaces is a type of software RAID that supports these forms of RAID:

- RAID 0 or spanning where multiple drives are strung together to allow for space on these drives to be managed as a single volume.

- RAID 1 or mirroring where data is duplicated on two drives to provide fault tolerance.

- RAID 5 or parity to improve performance and also provide fault tolerance without wasting space with redundant data.

> ⚡ **Caution** If you're thinking about using Storage Spaces to hold valuable data, remember that hardware RAID is generally considered much more stable and safer than software RAID.

> ❓ **To Learn More** To learn more about the types of RAID and how hardware and software RAID work, start at page 256 of Chapter 6 in *A+ Guide to Managing and Maintaining Your PC, 8th Edition*, and page 220 of Chapter 5 in *A+ Guide to Hardware, 6th Edition*.

▲ *Fast startup and new troubleshooting tools:* Windows 8 starts faster than previous Windows editions because, by default, it uses a fast startup feature similar to hibernation. It also offers new troubleshooting tools and techniques, several designed for ease of use for a technician to step a novice user through a process to repair, restore, refresh, or reset the Windows installation. The tools are designed so that a non-technical end user can solve even the most challenging Windows problems with only phone support. Chapter 3 focuses on how these tools work.

▲ *UEFI firmware support:* Windows 8 is designed to work well with UEFI firmware on its motherboard, which is slowly replacing BIOS as the firmware used to manage the hardware before Windows is loaded.

> ❓ **To Learn More** To learn more about booting a computer using BIOS or UEFI firmware, start at page 146 in Chapter 4 of *A+ Guide to Managing and Maintaining Your PC, 8th Edition*, and page 110 of Chapter 3 in *A+ Guide to Hardware, 6th Edition*.

◢ *Client Hyper-V:* Client Hyper-V is a desktop virtual machine manager that's an embedded feature of 64-bit Windows 8 Professional.

◢ *New Task Manager:* Task Manager gets a major overhaul and includes the ability to control startup processes, which previously belonged to the System Configuration utility (Msconfig).

◢ *Ongoing releases of the OS:* For operating systems prior to Windows 8, Microsoft releases service packs from time to time that include major updates to the OS. These service packs appear in the Windows Update window and are installed in a similar fashion to the way regular updates are installed. Windows 8 gets regular updates in this same way, but it doesn't receive service packs. Instead, Microsoft offers new releases of Windows 8 as free upgrades to the OS. The latest release of Windows 8 is Windows 8.1 and it applies to all editions of Windows 8.

Corporations often allow an employee to connect his or her desktop, laptop, smart phone, tablet, or other mobile device to the corporate network. The practice is called Bring Your Own Device (BYOD), and Windows 8 offers several features to make it easy for the IT department in a corporation to secure and support these devices. Here's a list of features in Windows 8 that support BYOD:

◢ *Windows to Go:* Windows 8 Enterprise offers Windows to Go, which can be used to create a Windows 8 installation on a bootable USB flash drive. A user can boot any computer from the flash drive to provide a fully secured corporate Windows 8 desktop.

◢ *Workplace Join:* The Workplace Join feature gives a user limited access to corporate resources on a domain without the computer having to join the domain. The user must register the device, and then the IT department can decide how much access the device has to domain resources. Part of these resources can be Work Folders. These folders are stored on the local device and will automatically sync up with Work Folders on the corporate servers when the device connects in a Workplace Join. Workplace Join and Work Folders are new with Windows 8.1.

◢ *Remote Business Data Removal:* Using the Remote Business Data Removal feature of Windows 8, data on a device can be tagged as corporate data and then can be wiped remotely if the device is stolen or the employee is no longer associated with the corporation. This feature is only available with Windows 8.1.

Now that you know a little of what's new with Windows 8, let's learn how to use it.

GETTING AROUND THE WINDOWS 8 INTERFACE AND THE WINDOWS DESKTOP

Although the architecture "under the hood" of Windows 8 hasn't changed much over Windows 7, the user interface certainly has. By default, when you first start up Windows 8 and get past the sign-in screen, the Windows 8 Start screen appears (refer back to Figure 1-1). (Later in the chapter, you'll learn how to configure Windows 8 to launch the desktop rather than the Start screen when you first start Windows.)

> 📝 **Notes** The instructions in this chapter assume that you are using a mouse and keyboard. If you're using a touch screen, simply tap instead of click; press and hold instead of right-click; double-tap instead of double-click; and swipe to scroll the screen to the right or left.

APPLYING CONCEPTS   SIGN IN TO WINDOWS 8 AND USE THE WINDOWS 8 INTERFACE

Although the Windows 8 interface is designed to work best with a touch screen, you can also use a mouse and keyboard. Follow these steps to learn how to sign in to Windows 8 and manage apps using the Windows 8 interface:

1. When you first start up a Windows 8 computer, you see the lock screen shown in Figure 1-4a. Click anywhere on the screen and the sign-in screen appears (see Figure 1-4b). To sign in, select a user account and enter the account password. The Start screen appears.

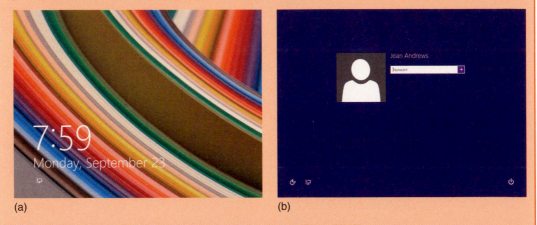

(a)   (b)

Figure 1-4   (a)The Windows lock screen, and (b) the Windows sign-in screen
Used with permission from Microsoft Corporation

2. To open an app, click the app tile on the Start screen. If the app works in the Windows 8 interface, the app page opens. (If the app works on the Windows desktop, the desktop appears and the app window opens.)

3. To return to the Start screen, press the **Win** key. Open a second app, which fills the entire screen.

> 📝 **Notes** In Windows, there are multiple ways to do the same thing. For example, to return to the Start screen (a) press the **Win** key, (b) move your pointer to the bottom left of the screen and click the **Start** (Windows logo) button that appears, or (c) move your pointer to a right corner of the screen and click the **Start** (Windows logo) charm in the charms bar that appears.

4. You can snap a page to the left or right side of the screen so a second page can share the screen. To snap a page, first move your pointer to the top of the screen—the pointer changes to a hand. Then press and drag the page down and to the left or right side of the screen. The page snaps to the side, and the second app takes up the other side of the screen. You can press and drag the vertical bar between the two pages to adjust the page sizes (see Figure 1-5).

> 📝 **Notes** To snap pages, your screen resolution must be at least 1366 × 768.

Figure 1-5 Two app pages show on the screen with other open apps shown as thumbnails in the left pane
Used with permission from Microsoft Corporation

Thumbnails of open apps not currently displayed

Drag the vertical bar to resize the two pages

5. Open three other apps using each of these three methods:

◢ If the app tile isn't showing, move your pointer to the bottom of the screen. You can then use the scroll bar that appears to scroll the screen to the right or left to see more apps on the Start screen. (You can also move your pointer to the far left or right side of the screen to scroll the screen.)

◢ Some apps are not on the Start screen. Move your pointer to the bottom of the Start screen and a down arrow appears. Click the **arrow** to see the Apps screen, which shows all installed apps (see Figure 1-6). Click one to open it.

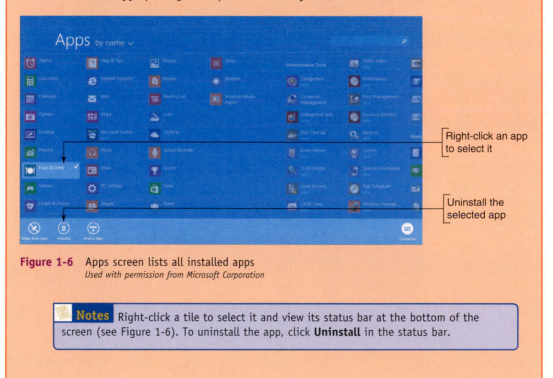

Right-click an app to select it

Uninstall the selected app

Figure 1-6 Apps screen lists all installed apps
Used with permission from Microsoft Corporation

📝 **Notes** Right-click a tile to select it and view its status bar at the bottom of the screen (see Figure 1-6). To uninstall the app, click **Uninstall** in the status bar.

▲ You can also use the Search feature to open an app. On the Start screen, start typing the name of the app. As you type, the Search pane appears. For example, in Figure 1-7, you can see the pane when *no* is typed. The remaining letters in *notepad* automatically appear in the search box, and other possibilities are listed in the pane. If you want to open the Notepad app, click it. By default, the Search app searches for apps, Windows settings, files, Web images, and Web videos. If you click an item at the bottom of the pane, Internet Explorer opens to find it on the Web.

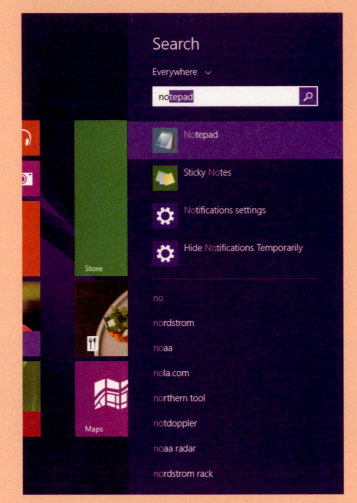

Figure 1-7   Use Search to search for apps, settings, files, and content within other apps and on the Web
Used with permission from Microsoft Corporation

6. Only two apps can use the screen at one time. To see thumbnails of open apps that are not on the screen, move your pointer to the upper-left corner of the screen (refer to Figure 1-5).

7. To close an app, move your pointer to the top of the screen. Your pointer changes to a hand. Press and drag the hand down to the bottom of the screen. (It's like pulling down a window shade. It's awkward, but it works fairly well when using a touch screen.) Close all open apps.

THE CHARMS BAR AND THE SETTINGS CHARM

The **charms bar** appears on the right side of any Windows 8 screen when you move your pointer to a right corner (see Figure 1-8a). It gives handy access to common tasks such as returning to the Start screen, searching for content, connecting to a wireless network, personalizing the Start screen, or changing other Windows settings. In the charms bar, click a charm to select it. The Settings charm can be particularly useful, and items at the top of the Settings pane can change depending on the situation. Figure 1-8b shows the Settings pane from the Start screen, and Figure 1-8c shows the Settings pane from the desktop.

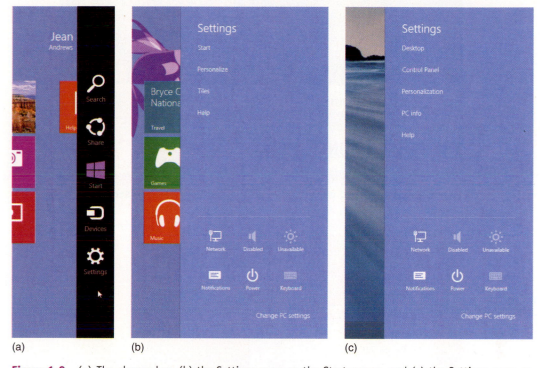

(a)   (b)   (c)

Figure 1-8   (a) The charms bar, (b) the Settings pane on the Start screen, and (c) the Settings pane on the desktop
Used with permission from Microsoft Corporation

> **Notes** With the first release of Windows 8, many users complained that important items like the charms bar were difficult to find and not at all intuitive to use. As a result, beginning with Windows 8.1, Microsoft added tips that randomly appear on screen to help users learn how to use the new interface.

THE SETTINGS CHARM AND THE POWER ICON

The Power icon in the Settings pane can be used to shut down or restart the computer. Click the **Power** icon, and then click an item in the menu that appears (see Figure 1-9). The items on this menu always include Shut down and Restart, and, depending on the configuration, might also include Sleep and Hibernate.

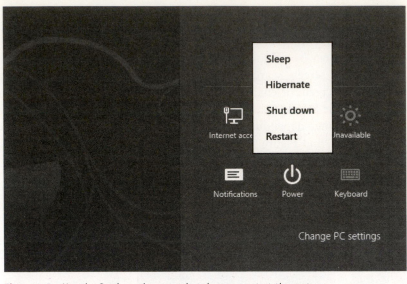

Figure 1-9 Use the Settings charm to shut down or restart the system
Used with permission from Microsoft Corporation

THE QUICK LAUNCH MENU

From anywhere in Windows, to get to several useful Windows utilities, press **Win+X**. The
Quick Launch menu, also called the WinX menu, opens (see Figure 1-10). Click an item to

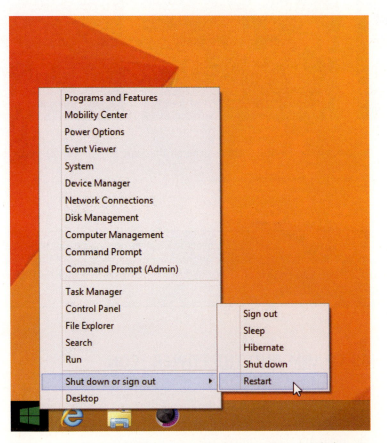

Figure 1-10 Use the Quick Launch menu from anywhere in Windows to
access useful Windows utilities and screens
Used with permission from Microsoft Corporation

open it. When using the desktop, you can also right-click the Start button in the taskbar to get to the Quick Launch menu.

Notice the *Shut down or sign out* item near the bottom of the menu. When you point to it, you see submenu items that always include Shut down, Sign out, and Restart. Depending on your system configuration, you might also see Sleep or Hibernate.

> 📒 **Notes** To change the options available in the *Shut down or sign out* menu or the Power icon in the Settings charm, click **Power Options** in the Quick Launch menu.

APPLYING | CONCEPTS   PRACTICE USING THE CHARMS BAR AND QUICK LAUNCH MENU

Do the following to practice using the charms bar and Quick Launch menu:

1. Open the **charms** bar, and then open the **Settings** charm. What are the options on the Power icon menu?

2. Open the **Quick Launch** menu, and practice using several options on the menu. What are the submenu items that appear when you point to *Shut down or sign out*?

3. Click **Power Options** on the Quick Launch menu. Find the settings in the Power Options window that allow you to change the options available in the *Shut down or sign out* menu.

4. Go to the **Start** screen. Click your user name in the top-right corner of the Start screen. What options appear in the dropdown menu? Use the Lock and Sign out options, and describe what each option does.

THE WINDOWS DESKTOP

To get to the traditional Windows desktop, click the **Desktop** tile on the Start screen. When you move your pointer to a right corner of the desktop screen, the charms bar appears as shown in Figure 1-11. Click the **Start** charm in the charms bar to return to the Start screen. Alternately, you can click the Start button in the taskbar to return to the Start screen.

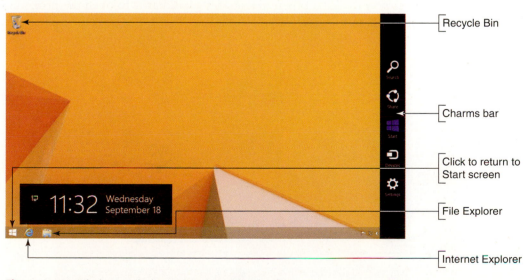

Recycle Bin

Charms bar

Click to return to Start screen

File Explorer

Internet Explorer

Figure 1-11 Windows 8 desktop with charms bar in view
Used with permission from Microsoft Corporation

Also in the taskbar are the Internet Explorer and File Explorer icons in the Quick Launch toolbar. IE version 10 is included with Windows 8, and IE version 11 comes with Windows 8.1.

The File Explorer (called Windows Explorer in Windows 7) window has tabs near the top of the window (see Figure 1-12). These tabs can change depending on the situation. You click a tab to see its ribbon or a dropdown menu that appears with more tools. The Computer ribbon is shown in the figure.

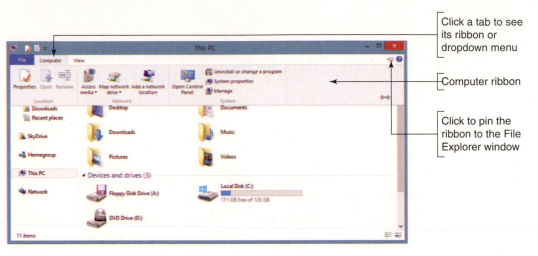

Click a tab to see its ribbon or dropdown menu

Computer ribbon

Click to pin the ribbon to the File Explorer window

Figure 1-12   File Explorer window with the Computer ribbon shown
Used with permission from Microsoft Corporation

To start a desktop application, you normally click the **Start** button to return to the Start screen and use the Start screen to open an app. For example, on the Start screen, start typing the name of the app, and then click it when it appears in the search list. If it's a desktop application, the program window launches on the desktop.

For a desktop program you use often, you can add its icon to the taskbar on the desktop. To do that, right-click an app on the Start screen or Apps screen to see the app's status bar at the bottom of the screen (refer back to Figure 1-6). If the app works on the desktop, the status bar includes the item *Pin to taskbar*.

Another way to add a program icon to the taskbar is to open the program, right-click the program's icon in the taskbar, and then click **Pin this program to taskbar** (see Figure 1-13).

Pin the application icon to the taskbar

Figure 1-13   Pin a program to the taskbar on the Windows desktop
Used with permission from Microsoft Corporation

You can also put a shortcut to a program on the desktop. To do so, first locate the program file stored in a subfolder in the C:\Program Files folder or the C:\Program Files (x86) folder. Right-click the program file, and click **Create shortcut**. Then click **Yes**. A shortcut to the program is created on the desktop.

APPLYING | CONCEPTS   INSTALL AND UNINSTALL WINDOWS 8 APPS

Windows 8 apps are installed from the Windows Store, and you must have a Microsoft account to do so. If you don't already have an account, you can get one free at live.com. Follow these steps to use a Microsoft account to install an app and then uninstall it:

1. If you don't already have a Microsoft account, go to the Windows desktop, open Internet Explorer, and go to **signup.live.com**. To create the account, you can use an existing email address (for example, someone@sample.edu) or request a new email address, which will be an outlook.com, hotmail.com, or live.com address. You'll need to enter your name, gender, and birth date, and, for security purposes, you'll need to associate a cell phone number and/or an alternate email address with the account. Be sure you write down your email address and password for your Microsoft account.

   Notes There's a bug in Windows 8 that sometimes gives errors when you try to access Facebook and other social networking sites using your Microsoft account that has an email address other than an outlook.com address. For this reason, if you plan to heavily use social networking sites while signed in to Windows 8 using your Microsoft account, set up the account using an outlook.com email address.

2. After you have created your account, close your browser, and return to the Start screen.

3. To install an app, click the **Store** tile. Next, scroll through the apps in the Store or use its search box to find an app (see Figure 1-14). Click a free one, and follow the directions on screen to install it. If you did not sign in to Windows using a Microsoft account, you are asked to sign in.

Figure 1-14   Search the Windows Store for apps to install
Used with permission from Microsoft Corporation

4. Practice using the app to make sure it works.

5. To uninstall the app, right-click the app tile on the Start screen or Apps screen. The status bar at the bottom of the screen shows options available for the app, including Uninstall (refer back to Figure 1-6). Click **Uninstall**, and follow the directions on screen.

You have just seen how you can sign in to the Windows Store using a Microsoft account. You can also use the account to sign in to Windows 8. When you do so, you are automatically signed in to the Windows Store as well as other online resources. Now let's see how all this works.

USE A MICROSOFT ACCOUNT TO SIGN IN TO WINDOWS 8

Windows 8 offers three ways to sign in to Windows:

1. A local account to sign in to the local computer

2. A domain account to sign in to Windows and authenticate to a Windows domain

3. A Microsoft account, which is linked to an email address that allows you to access several types of online accounts including Microsoft SkyDrive, Facebook, LinkedIn, Twitter, Outlook.com, and others.

Windows 7 supports a local account and a domain account, and a Microsoft account is new to Windows 8. An email address is used to set up a Microsoft account on the live.com website. When you set up the account on the site, the account is assigned a SkyDrive, which is 7 GBs of free storage space in the cloud. You can pay for additional storage, and you can also use Microsoft's free cloud apps to manage data files stored on your SkyDrive.

WHY USE A MICROSOFT ACCOUNT WITH WINDOWS 8?

There are several advantages of signing in to Windows using a Microsoft account, including:

◢ When you use the same Microsoft account to sign in to multiple computers, your personal settings follow you to each computer, including your themes, Internet Explorer favorites, and language preferences.

◢ Apps you buy from the Windows Store can be installed on up to five Windows 8 computers and Windows RT mobile devices that are set up to use your Microsoft account.

◢ Windows automatically signs you in to your SkyDrive, Facebook, LinkedIn, Mail, or other online accounts that are set up with this email address. SkyDrive is embedded in many features of Windows 8. For example, you can see it listed in the left pane of File Explorer (refer back to Figure 1-12).

If you sign in to Windows with a local account or domain account and attempt to open the SkyDrive app, People app, Mail app, or other apps on the Start screen that require signing in online, an error message appears that offers to help you set up a Microsoft account for this computer (see Figure 1-15). You can, however, still access these online accounts through a browser. For example, you can open Internet Explorer, go to the live.com site, and sign in to your SkyDrive. Figure 1-16 diagrams two options for accessing your SkyDrive.

Figure 1-15 Apps on the Start screen that use a Microsoft account require you to switch to a Microsoft account when signing in to Windows 8
Used with permission from Microsoft Corporation

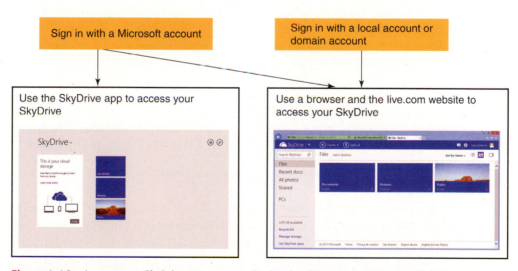

Figure 1-16 Access your SkyDrive storage area in the cloud by using either the SkyDrive app or the live.com website
Used with permission from Microsoft Corporation

A disadvantage of using your Microsoft account to sign in to Windows is that your private settings and access to your apps and online accounts are stored on the local computer. Therefore, you would only want to set up your Microsoft account on a computer where you trust those with administrative access to the computer. For many, this means using a Microsoft account only on your own personal computers that are under your complete control.

HOW TO USE A MICROSOFT ACCOUNT FOR SIGNING IN TO WINDOWS 8

Here are the ways you can set up a Microsoft account to sign in to Windows:

▲ *During the Windows installation:* When you first install Windows, you can provide an existing Microsoft account that is used to complete the installation. If you don't already have a Microsoft account, the setup process gives you the opportunity to create one.

▲ *Set up a new user account:* When you set up a new user account, you can make that account a Microsoft account. You'll learn how to set up new user accounts in the next section.

▲ *Connect an existing user account to a Microsoft account:* After the installation, you can use the Settings charm to connect an existing local account or domain account to a Microsoft account.

> **Notes** To connect a domain account to a Microsoft account, Group Policies controlling the Windows domain must allow it. After the connection, the Microsoft account is used to authenticate to the domain.

TRUSTED DEVICES FOR YOUR MICROSOFT ACCOUNT

When you manage the security settings associated with your Microsoft account or access sensitive information about the account, Microsoft asks you to verify your identity by sending a security code to your cell phone or the alternate email address associated with the account. You must retrieve the code from your cell phone or email and enter it on a page at live.com in order to prove your identity. To bypass this process, you can designate a computer as a trusted device. When you do so, Microsoft will not require the code when you use the trusted computer to manage your Microsoft account. You are given the opportunity to designate a computer as a trusted device when you convert a local or domain account to a Microsoft account and you can also designate the computer as a trusted device at any time by using the Settings charm. Both methods are covered in this chapter.

APPLYING CONCEPTS   CONVERT A LOCAL OR DOMAIN ACCOUNT TO A MICROSOFT ACCOUNT

Follow these steps to convert a local account or a domain account to a Microsoft account:

1. Sign in to Windows using your local or domain account, and then open the **charms** bar, click the **Settings** charm, and click **Change PC settings**. Click **Accounts**. If necessary, click **Your account**, and then click **Connect to a Microsoft account** (see Figure 1-17).

2. The screen shown in Figure 1-18 appears where you can enter information for an existing Microsoft account or start the process of creating a new account. Make your choice, and follow directions on screen.

3. At one point in the process, the screen in Figure 1-19 appears where you are given the opportunity to receive a security code from Microsoft that you can use to make your computer a trusted device. To receive the code on your cell phone or alternate email address, click **Next**. If you already have received the code, click **I have a code**. If you want to skip this step and not make the computer a trusted device, click **I can't do this right now**. Continue following the on screen directions.

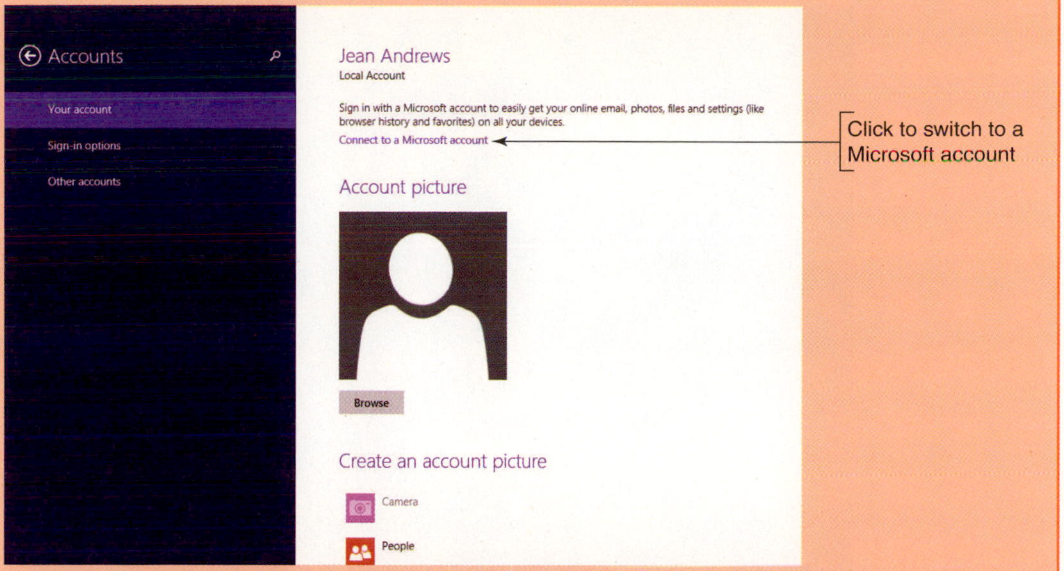

1

Figure 1-17 Use the Accounts screen to connect a local account to a Microsoft account
Used with permission from Microsoft Corporation

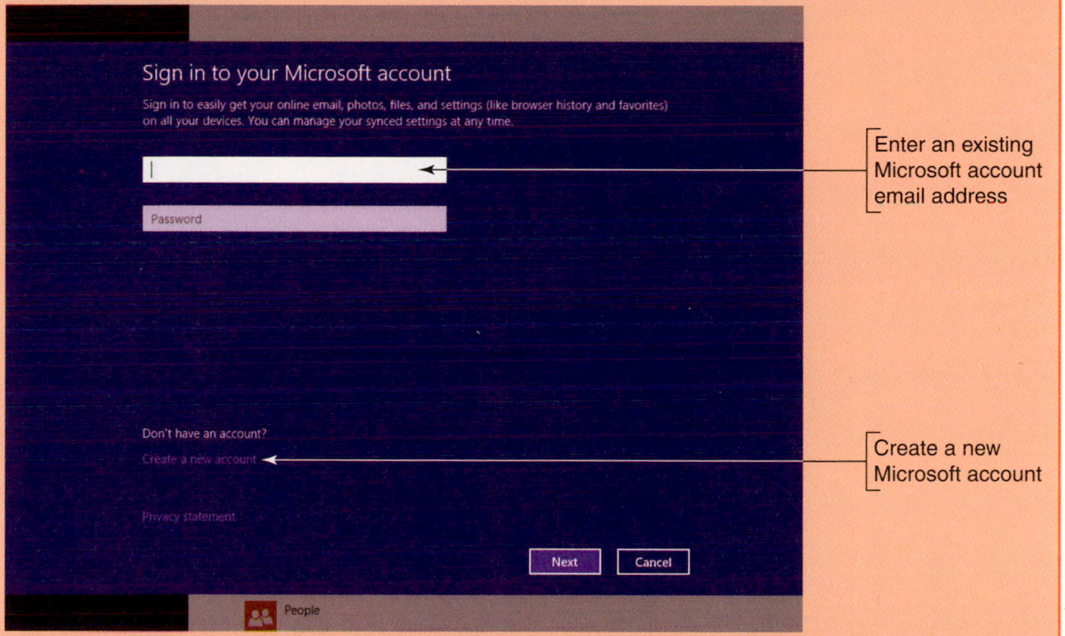

Figure 1-18 Set up an existing Microsoft account or create a new account that will be used for signing in to Windows
Used with permission from Microsoft Corporation

4. The last screen in the process is shown in Figure 1-20. Click **Switch** to complete the process.

5. Sign out of Windows and sign back in using your Microsoft account and password.

When you sign in to Windows using a Microsoft account, your Windows personal settings, IE favorites, and apps installed from the Windows Store are synced with up to five computers you use. You can control what gets synced and other security settings—how to do so is coming up.

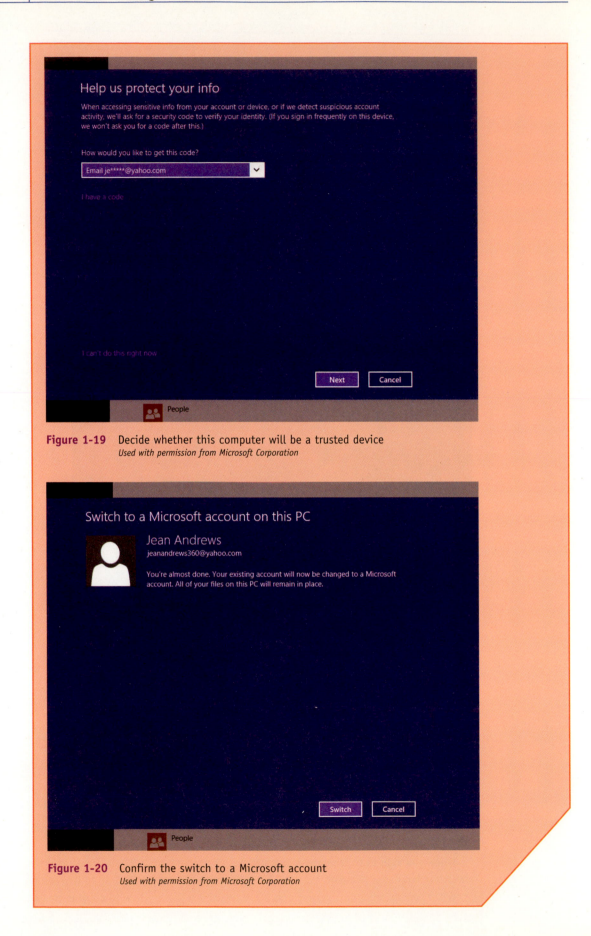

Figure 1-19   Decide whether this computer will be a trusted device
Used with permission from Microsoft Corporation

Figure 1-20   Confirm the switch to a Microsoft account
Used with permission from Microsoft Corporation

CHANGE YOUR MICROSOFT ACCOUNT PASSWORD AND OTHER ACCOUNT SECURITY SETTINGS

If you sign in to Windows with a Microsoft account, your computer must be connected to the Internet to change your Microsoft account password and other account security settings because this information is kept online. One way to manage these settings is to use a browser to go to live.com and sign in to your Microsoft account. You can then change security settings including your password and the billing information used to purchase apps from the Windows Store. This method works from any computer, including those that are not Windows 8 computers or Windows 8 computers that don't use your Microsoft account for signing in.

Another way to manage your Microsoft account settings is to use the Settings charm in Windows 8. To use this method, the Windows 8 computer that uses your Microsoft account must first be designated as a trusted device.

DESIGNATE A COMPUTER AS A TRUSTED DEVICE

To designate a computer that uses your Microsoft account to be a trusted device, follow these steps:

1. Open the **Settings** charm, go to the **PC settings** screen, and click **Accounts**. If necessary, click **Your account** (see Figure 1-21). If the computer has not yet been designated as a trusted device, you see the Verify link that is used to verify your identity on this computer, as shown in Figure 1-21.

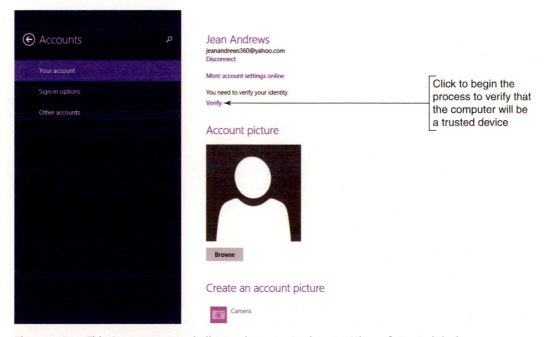

Figure 1-21 This Accounts screen indicates the computer is not a Microsoft trusted device
Used with permission from Microsoft Corporation

2. Click **Verify**. On the following screens, you'll be asked to verify your identity on the computer by clicking a link in an email message sent to you or by entering a security code sent to your cell phone. Follow directions on screen. When you are finished, the Verify link is missing from the Your account screen, which tells you that the computer is now a trusted device.

3. To edit the account settings, click **More account settings online**. Two pages appear on your screen (see Figure 1-22). The Internet Explorer page on the right shows the Microsoft account settings at live.com for your account. Click links on the left side of this page to see information on the right side of the page. Using these links, you can change your password, personal info, security info, and billing information. You can also close the account. To remove all trusted devices associated with this account, click **Security info** on the left, click **Remove all the trusted devices associated with my account** on the right, and follow directions on screen.

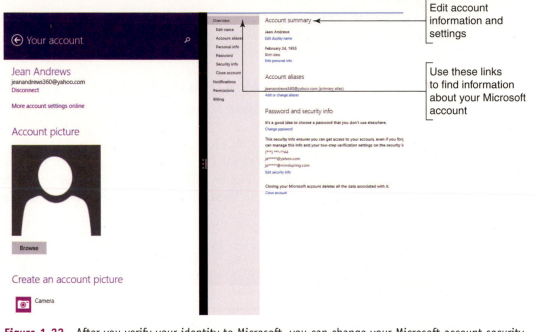

Figure 1-22   After you verify your identity to Microsoft, you can change your Microsoft account security settings
Used with permission from Microsoft Corporation

After you have verified your identity, you can return to the Your account pane to change Microsoft account settings and information without having to reidentify yourself as the owner of the account. To do so, click **More account settings online**, and sign in to your Microsoft account.

> ⚡ **Caution**   Don't designate a computer as a trusted PC unless you are its only user or you trust all users who have admin rights to the computer. If you share the PC with other users, be aware that they can reset your password and potentially hijack your Microsoft account.

MANAGE MICROSOFT ACCOUNT SYNC SETTINGS

After a computer is designated as a trusted device, you can manage the sync settings for your Microsoft account. These settings apply to all devices that use your Microsoft account for signing in. Open the **charms** bar, click **Settings**, and click **Change PC settings**. In the PC Settings pane, click **SkyDrive, Sync settings** (see Figure 1-23). Scroll down the page to see all the settings including Personalization settings, App settings, Back up settings, and other settings such as IE favorites, language preferences, and printer settings.

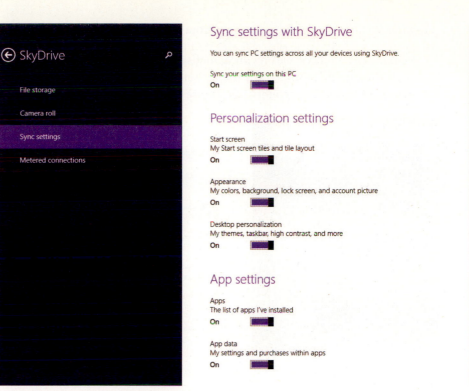

Figure 1-23 Decide what to sync on each computer that uses your Microsoft account
Used with permission from Microsoft Corporation

DISCONNECT A MICROSOFT ACCOUNT FROM WINDOWS 8 SIGN-IN

If you want to switch the user account on a Windows 8 computer from a Microsoft account back to a local account or domain account, use the **charms** bar to go to the **PC settings** screen, click **Accounts**, and click **Disconnect** (refer back to Figure 1-21).

SET UP AND MANAGE USER ACCOUNTS

In Windows 8, you can set up new user accounts (local accounts or Microsoft accounts) to be used to sign in to Windows on the local computer. (For a Microsoft account, you must be connected to the Internet when you set up the account.) In Windows 7, a user account can be set up as a standard account or an administrator account. In Windows 8, a user account can be set up as an administrator account, standard account, or child account. A child account is new to Windows 8 and gives parents extra control over what a child can do with the system and the Web, and sends reports to parents about the account activities.

SET UP A NEW USER ACCOUNT

In Windows 8, you can create a new account using the Settings charm, and you can also create accounts using the Computer Management console, as is done in Windows 7.

> **? To Learn More** To learn more about using the Computer Management console to create user accounts, start at page 836 of Chapter 17 in *A+ Guide to Managing and Maintaining Your PC, 8th Edition*, and page 384 of Chapter 8 in *A+ Guide to Software, 6th Edition*.

To use the Settings charm to create an account, do the following:

1. Sign in to Windows 8 using an administrator account. Open the **Settings** charm, and click **Change PC settings**. On the PC settings screen, click **Accounts**. On the Accounts screen, click **Other accounts** (see Figure 1-24).

Figure 1-24 Set up a new user account
Used with permission from Microsoft Corporation

2. Click **Add an account**. The *How will this person sign in?* screen appears (see Figure 1-25) where you have four options:

   ◢ To set up an existing Microsoft account on this computer, enter the email address for the account, and click **Next**.
   ◢ To sign up for a new email address that will also be a Microsoft account, click **Sign up for a new email address**.
   ◢ To set up a child account, click **Add a child's account**.
   ◢ To set up a local account, click **Sign in without a Microsoft account (not recommended)**, and click **Next**.

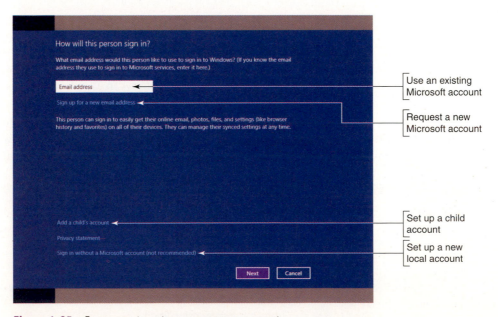

Figure 1-25 Four ways to set up a new user account
Used with permission from Microsoft Corporation

3. Follow directions on screen to set up the account. Figure 1-26 shows the next screen that appears when you're setting up a child account. Notice you can create the account with or without an email address. If the account is connected to an email address (which means it is a Microsoft account), you can go online to control online permissions for the account.

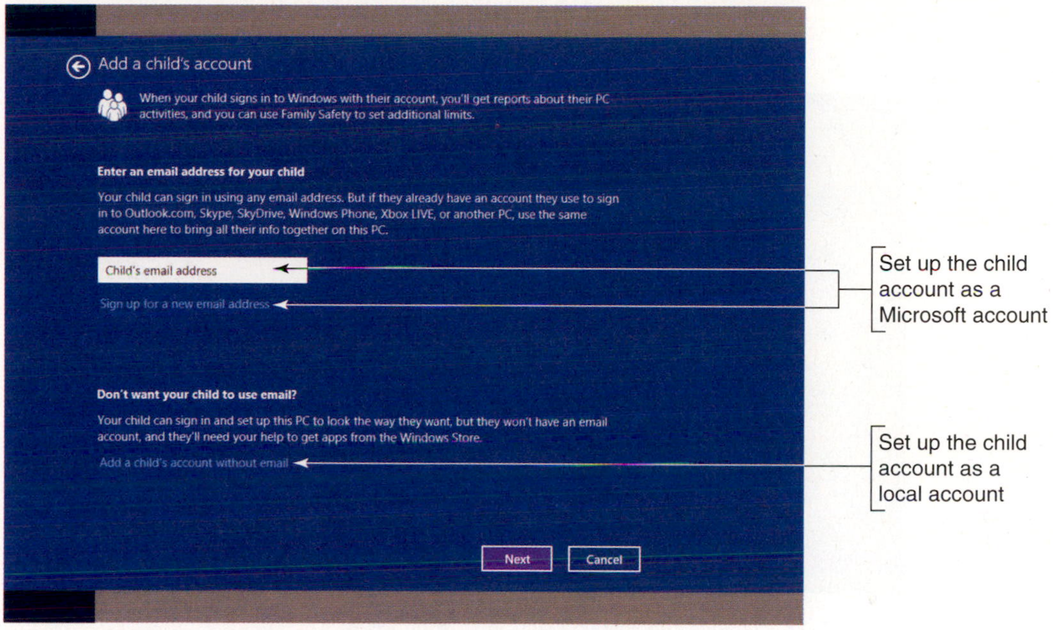

Figure 1-26 Set up a child account
Used with permission from Microsoft Corporation

REMOVE AN ACCOUNT OR CHANGE THE ACCOUNT TYPE

By default, a new account is a Standard user account. Later, if you want to remove an account or change the account type (for example, to make a standard user account an administrator account), return to the Accounts screen, and click **Other accounts**.

To remove an account, click the account, and click **Remove**. To edit the account type, select the account, and click **Edit**. In the Edit account pane, you can change the account type to an Administrator, Standard User, or Child account (see Figure 1-27).

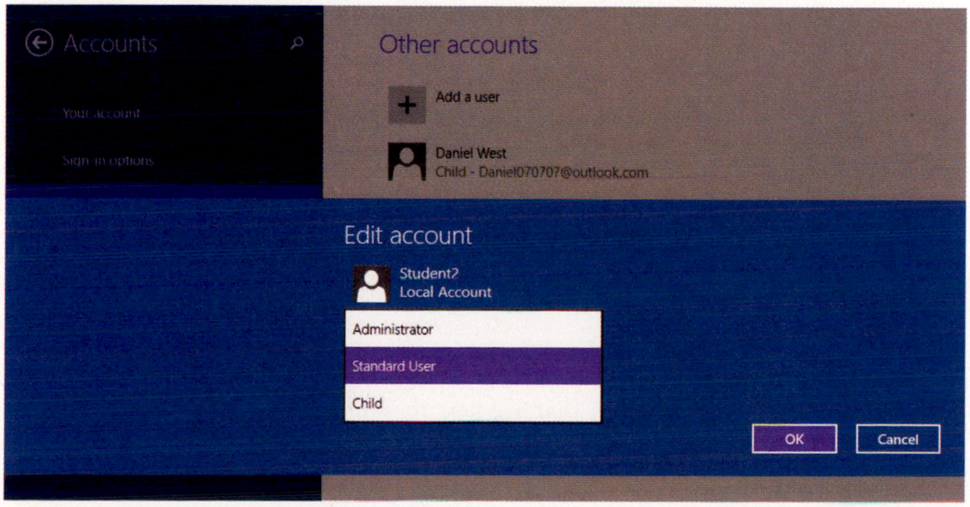

Figure 1-27 Use the Settings charm to change an account type
Used with permission from Microsoft Corporation

CHANGE YOUR SIGN-IN PASSWORD

To change the password to your user account, go to the **Accounts** screen, and click **Sign-in options**. On this screen (see Figure 1-28) you can change your password, set up a picture password, or set up a four-digit personal identification number (PIN) to quickly sign in to Windows. A picture password is new to Windows 8, and is designed for a touch screen. You select a picture and also select a particular swipe on the picture to sign in to Windows.

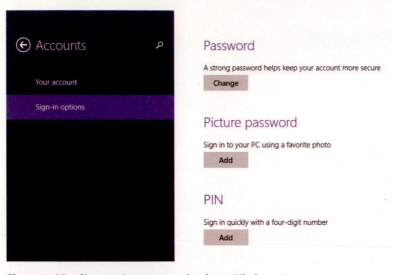

Figure 1-28 Change the way you sign in to Windows 8
Used with permission from Microsoft Corporation

> 📝 **Notes** When you change your password for a Microsoft account, your computer must be connected to the Internet because the password is stored online.

RESET THE PASSWORD FOR ANOTHER USER'S ACCOUNT

To reset a forgotten password for a local account other than your own, sign in as an administrator, press **Win+X**, and click **Computer Management**. In the Computer Management window that opens on the desktop, drill down to the list of user accounts under Local Users and Groups in the System Tools group. Right-click the user account, and click **Set Password**. Then follow directions on screen.

> 📝 **Notes** Any encrypted data in a user's profile will be lost when the user's password is reset by an administrator.

>> CHAPTER SUMMARY

What's New with Windows 8

- ◢ Features for the end user that are new to Windows 8 include the Start screen, the Windows 8 interface, the SkyDrive native app, Windows Store, sign in with a Microsoft account, and File History.

- ◢ Features for the technician to support Windows 8 include Windows 8 ARM support for mobile devices, Storage Spaces, fast startup, several troubleshooting tools, improved UEFI firmware support, Client Hyper-V, a new Task Manager, and a new way to release Windows 8 major updates.

◢ Features specifically designed for corporate use are Windows to Go, Workplace Join, Work Folders, and Remote Business Data Removal.

Getting Around the Windows 8 Interface and the Windows Desktop

◢ Use tiles on the Start screen to open applications. In the Windows 8 interface, only two app pages can appear on a screen at one time.

◢ Windows 8 search finds apps, settings, files, and content in files and on the Web.

◢ The charms bar includes several charms to manage the OS. The Settings charm is useful for changing many Windows settings and for restarting or shutting down the computer.

◢ The Windows desktop works as it does with previous Windows editions except the Start button takes you to the Start screen where you can launch applications. When a desktop app is launched from the Start screen, its window appears on the desktop.

◢ Use Win+X to access the Quick Launch menu that you can use to get to several useful Windows tools, including the Computer Management console, Control Panel, System window, and Event Viewer.

◢ You can sign in to Windows using a local account, domain account, or Microsoft account.

◢ A Microsoft account set up at live.com includes free cloud storage called a SkyDrive. The Microsoft account password and other settings for the account are managed online at live.com.

◢ When you sign in with a Microsoft account, you have access to other online accounts associated with your Microsoft account, and your personal settings and Windows 8 apps can follow you from one computer to another.

◢ You can connect a local account or a domain account to a Microsoft account, and you can disconnect the Microsoft account from the local or domain account.

◢ Windows supports three types of user accounts: administrator account, standard user account, and child account. A parent can control what a child account can do on the computer and online and can get email reports about the child account activity.

◢ Use the Settings charm or the Computer Management console to set up a new user account and manage user accounts.

◢ You can make it easier to sign in to Windows by assigning a picture password to a touch-screen device or assigning a four-digit PIN to be used in place of the password to a user account.

>> KEY TERMS

charms bar – A bar on the right side of the screen that works from anywhere in Windows to give handy access to common tasks such as connecting to a wireless network.

child account – A user account type that gives parents extra control over what a child can do with the system and sends a report to parents about the account activities.

Client Hyper-V – A virtual machine manager included in 64-bit Windows 8 Professional.

File History – An easy-to-use tool for backing up personal data stored on the hard drive.

live tile – A tile on the Start screen that offers continuous real-time updates.

Microsoft account – An account set up at live.com associated with an email address that allows you to access several types of online accounts including Microsoft SkyDrive, Facebook, LinkedIn, Twitter, Outlook.com, and others.

picture password – A type of password designed for a touch screen that uses a particular picture and user-designated swipe across the picture to gain access to the OS.

Quick Launch menu – From anywhere in Windows, press **Win+X** to see a menu of useful Windows utilities. You can also view the menu when you right-click the **Start** button on the desktop. Also called the WinX menu.

Remote Business Data Removal – A feature of Windows 8.1 that allows technical support to remotely delete corporate data from a device in the event the device is lost or stolen.

sideloading – Illegally installing apps without using the Windows Store.

SkyDrive – Cloud storage associated with a Microsoft account; the first 7 GB is free. Windows 8 is designed to fully integrate with a user's SkyDrive to make it easy to store data in the cloud.

Start screen – The screen that appears after signing in and is used to start an application. Apps on the Start screen are represented as tiles.

Storage Spaces – A type of software RAID included in Windows 8 that is used to manage multiple drives installed in the computer.

trusted device – In Windows 8, a computer recognized by Microsoft as one that can be trusted to change online security settings for your Microsoft account without verifying that you are the owner of the account.

Windows 8 interface – A user interface that uses pages for apps rather than windows used on the older Windows desktop.

Windows 8.1 – The latest release of Windows 8. It applies to all editions of Windows 8.

Windows RT – An edition of Windows 8 that supports an ARM processor and chipset hardware architecture used on many smart phones, tablets, and other mobile devices.

Windows Store – A Microsoft website that is also an app on the Start screen used to purchase and download apps that use the Windows 8 interface.

Windows to Go – A feature of Windows 8 Enterprise, which can be used to create a Windows 8 installation on a bootable USB flash drive. When you boot from the drive, a fully secured corporate Windows 8 desktop can be installed on an employee's personal computer.

Work Folders – Folders stored on the local device that will automatically sync with Work Folders on the corporate servers when the device connects in a Workplace Join.

Workplace Join – A Windows 8.1 feature that gives a user limited access to corporate resources on a domain without the computer having to join the domain.

>> REVIEWING THE BASICS

1. What are the two user interfaces included with Windows 8?

2. Which of the two interfaces uses pages instead of windows to display open apps?

3. To conserve system resources, how can you turn off a live tile so it does not continually update?

4. How much free cloud storage does a SkyDrive have?

5. Which app do you use on the Start screen to install new apps?

6. Which edition of Windows 8 is designed specifically to support ARM processors?

7. What feature of Windows 8 can you use to span a single volume across two hard drives?

8. Major updates to Windows 7 are published as service packs. How are major updates to Windows 8 published?

9. Which feature of Windows 8 allows corporate data to be wiped from a device that has been lost or stolen?

10. Which Windows 8 feature is used to boot a computer to Windows 8 when Windows is installed on a bootable USB flash drive?

11. Which Windows 8.1 feature is used to sync folders stored on a local device with those stored on a corporate server?

12. In the Windows 8 interface, how many pages can be displayed on a screen?

13. Where on the screen does Windows 8 display thumbnails of open apps when the app page is currently not displayed on screen?

14. List the steps to uninstall an app that uses the Windows 8 interface.

15. Which version of Internet Explorer is included with Windows 8? With Windows 8.1?

16. Which keys do you press to open the Quick Launch menu?

17. List three ways to sign in to Windows 8.

18. List three types of user accounts available in Windows 8.

19. Which charm can you use to set up a new user account?

20. What appears when you right-click the Start button on the desktop?

>> THINKING CRITICALLY

1. Suppose you have purchased and installed apps from the Windows Store on your home computer using your Microsoft account. At work, you connect your Microsoft account to your domain account to sign in to your work computer. Will the apps installed on your home computer now be installed on your work computer? Select the best answer.

   a. No, because apps from the Windows Store are only installed on the device where they were originally purchased.

   b. Yes, because apps purchased with your Microsoft account are installed on up to five computers you sign in to using this account.

   c. No, because syncing apps to all computers that use your Microsoft account is disabled by default.

   d. Yes, because when you purchase an app from the Windows Store, you can designate that app be synced with all computers that use your Microsoft account.

   e. No, because apps can never be synced on work computers that belong to a Windows domain.

2. Suppose you sign in to Windows with a local account. You go to the **PC settings** screen, click **SkyDrive**, and then click **Sync settings**. Why do you think you find these settings are gray and not available?

   a. Sync settings apply only when a Microsoft account is used to sign in to Windows.

   b. Sync settings are available only if enabled in Control Panel.

   c. Sync settings apply only when a computer has joined a domain.

   d. Sync settings can be viewed but not edited on the PC settings screen. To edit them, use Control Panel.

3. A user clicks the SkyDrive app on the Start screen, and Windows requests the user's Microsoft account and password. Which of the following statements are true?

   a. Another user has used the SkyDrive app on this computer.

   b. This is the first time the user has opened the SkyDrive app.

   c. The user doesn't have a Microsoft account.

   d. The user did not sign in to Windows using a Microsoft account.

>> HANDS-ON PROJECTS

PROJECT 1-1:   Using Windows 8

Practice using Windows 8 by doing the following:

1. Open four apps that use the Windows 8 interface. Practice moving from one open app to another. Then close all the apps.

2. Change the background picture or color on the Start screen.

3. Use the **Windows Store** to install a free app. Make sure the app works.

4. Use the **Quick Launch** menu to open the Programs and Features window. How many programs that use the desktop are installed on this computer?

5. Close the Programs and Features menu, and return to the **Start** screen. Open the **Notepad** app. Does this app use the desktop or the Windows 8 interface? Close Notepad.

6. Display the **Apps** screen. Is the Administrative Tools group of apps listed on the screen? Open the **Settings** charm, and click **Tiles**. Use the Tiles pane to show administrative tools. Return to the **Apps** screen, and make sure the Administrative Tools group is listed.

PROJECT 1-2:   Set up a Microsoft Account and Use SkyDrive

Do the following to practice using a Microsoft account and SkyDrive:

1. Sign in to Windows using a local account. Open the **Store** app on the Start screen, and try to install a free app. Windows won't allow you to do this unless you sign in to the Store using a Microsoft account.

2. Try to open the **SkyDrive** app on the Start screen. Windows won't allow you to do this unless you first switch the local account to a Microsoft account.

3. If you don't already have a Microsoft account, sign up for one.

4. Use the live.com website to create a new folder on your SkyDrive, and then upload a file to the folder. Any file will do.

5. Connect your local account to your Microsoft account, sign out, and sign back in to Windows using the Microsoft account. You can now use the SkyDrive app on the Start screen.

6. Open the **SkyDrive** app, and find the file on your SkyDrive. Download the file to your Windows desktop. Verify the file is on your desktop. Did Windows request your Microsoft account and password when you first opened the SkyDrive app?

7. Install a free app from the **Windows Store** on your Start screen. Which app did you install?

8. If you're working in a computer lab, disconnect your Microsoft account from the local account.

PROJECT 1-3: Use the Skype App

Skype-to-Skype calls are free from anywhere in the world and are a great way to communicate with friends in faraway places. Working with a partner using a different computer, use a microphone and the Skype app on the Start screen to make a voice call to your partner. If you don't already have a Skype account, set up a free account.

PROJECT 1-4: Practice Customizing the Start Screen

When learning to use a new OS, the Web can be a great resource. Search the Web to find out how to do the following, and then practice these skills in Windows 8:

1. Resize tiles on the Start screen.

2. Move tiles on the Start screen.

3. Select three or four tiles that you use the most, and create a new group for these tiles. Name this new group **My Favorite Apps**. Move this group to the far left side of the Start screen.

4. Pin a tile to the Start screen that is currently on the Apps screen. Then remove the tile from the Start screen. (Don't uninstall the app.)

5. Change the background color of the Start screen.

6. Change the picture that shows on your Lock screen (the screen that appears before you sign in to Windows).

>> REAL PROBLEMS, REAL SOLUTIONS

REAL PROBLEM 1-1: Document How to Use Windows 8

This real problem requires a microphone, and a web cam would also be useful. Make a screen recording with voice-over to teach end users how to use Windows 8. Do the following:

1. Screencast-O-Matic offers free software to make a screen recording with voice and video. Go to **screencast-o-matic.com**, and download and install the video recording software. As you follow directions to install the software, you might be required to also download and install Java.

2. Select a Windows 8 feature to explain. For example, you can explain how to customize the Start screen, open and close an app, install or uninstall an app, create a new user account, empty the Recycle Bin, or use the charms bar or search feature. You or your instructor might have other ideas.

3. Use the Screencast-O-Matic software to make a screen recording to show how to use the Windows 8 feature you selected. The recording should be no longer than 3 minutes. Explain the steps as you go. The software records your screen movements, your voice (if a microphone is detected), and video (if a web cam is detected).

4. View the video. If you see a problem, record it again. When you're satisfied with your video, save it as an MP4 file.

REAL PROBLEM 1-2: Launch the Desktop at Startup

Some users prefer to go directly to the Windows desktop rather than to the Start screen at Windows startup. To make this change, you'll need Windows 8.1 installed. Go to the Windows desktop, right-click the taskbar, and click **Properties**. In the Taskbar and Navigation properties box, click the **Navigation** tab (see Figure 1-29). Check **Go to the desktop instead of Start when I sign in**. Apply your changes. When you next sign in to Windows, you are taken directly to the desktop.

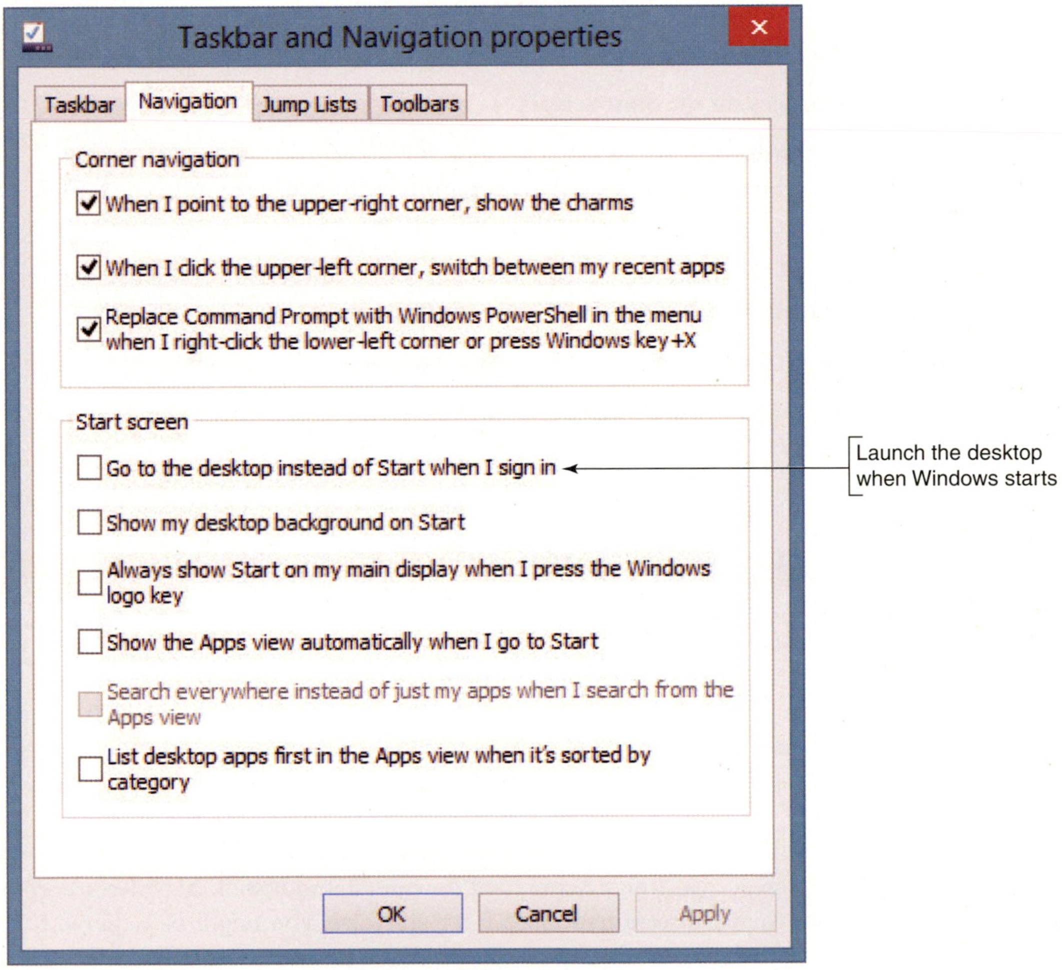

Figure 1-29 Control what happens when you navigate Windows 8
Used with permission from Microsoft Corporation

Installing Windows 8

When you learn to support a new OS, one of the first skills you'll learn is how to install it. In this chapter you'll first learn about the editions of Windows 8 and how to install it as an upgrade, clean install, and dual boot. You also learn what to do after an installation and how to upgrade Windows 8 to Windows 8.1. The chapter finishes with an introduction to Client Hyper-V, which is a feature of Windows 8 Professional that can be used to manage virtual machines on the desktop.

This chapter focuses on installations done by a technician working at the desktop, which are called high-touch with retail media installations. If you need to know about other types of installations, including creating and using a standard image, using a distribution share, and high-volume deployments of Windows 8, see the *Basic Windows Deployment Step-by-Step Guide* at technet.microsoft.com/library/hh825212.aspx.

> **Notes** Labs to accompany this chapter can be found in Lab B near the back of this book.

> **Notes** This chapter is written to follow Chapter 7 in *A+ Guide to Managing and Maintaining Your PC, 8th Edition*, or Chapter 2 in *A+ Guide to Software, 6th Edition*.

INSTALLING WINDOWS 8

In this part of the chapter, you learn about the minimum requirements for Windows 8, the editions of Windows 8, and how to perform an upgrade and clean install. You also learn about what to do after the installation.

MINIMUM HARDWARE REQUIREMENTS

Here are the minimum hardware requirements needed to install and run Windows 8:

▲ *Processor:* 1 GHz or faster with support for NX, PAE, and SSE2
▲ *Memory:* 1 GB for a 32-bit installation and 2 GB for a 64-bit installation
▲ *Hard disk free space:* 16 GB for a 32-bit installation and 20 GB for a 64-bit installation
▲ *Video card or onboard graphics:* Must support DirectX9 with WDDM driver

You might notice that these are the same minimum requirements for Windows 7 except for the three technologies used by the processor (NX, PAE, and SSE2). The three technologies were first used by processors about 10 years ago. By requiring the use of these technologies, Microsoft prevents Windows 8 from being installed on computers that are older than about 10 years. Next, let's see what these three processor technologies do for us.

NX (NEVER EXECUTE OR NO EXECUTE)

NX (Never Execute or No Execute) technology helps prevent malware from hiding and executing in the data storage area of another program. When the NX bit is turned on for a range of memory, malware stored in this range can't execute. NX has been included with most Intel and AMD processors since 2004. Intel calls the NX technology Execute Disable Bit (XD Bit), AMD calls it Enhanced Virus Protection (EVP), and ARM manufacturers calls it Execute Never (XN).

BIOS on a motherboard is used to enable/disable the NX feature in a processor (see Figure 2-1). Most boards built since 2004 support NX, and you can add the NX feature to BIOS by flashing BIOS.

To protect a system against malware, Windows 8 requires NX to be enabled and will not install otherwise. If the NX feature is disabled in BIOS, Windows 8 setup attempts to enable it during the installation.

PAE (PHYSICAL ADDRESS EXTENSION)

For a processor to support NX when it is running in 32-bit mode, it must use a processor feature called PAE (Physical Address Extension) in order to access the memory addresses required by NX. PAE was originally designed to allow a 32-bit processor to use more than 4 GB of RAM and is currently supported by all Intel and AMD processors that can run in 32-bit mode. Beginning with Windows XP Service Pack 2, PAE was not allowed to access more than 4 GB of RAM because it caused some device drivers to become unstable, but it is used for other OS activities including NX. PAE is always enabled in a processor, and, therefore, is not managed by BIOS setup. It is also enabled in Windows by default.

> **? To Learn More** Recall that all Intel and AMD processors sold today for desktop or notebook computers are hybrid processors and can support 32-bit or 64-bit processing. For more information about these processors, start at page 174 in Chapter 5 of *A+ Guide to Managing and Maintaining Your PC, 8th Edition*, or page 138 in Chapter 4 of *A+ Guide to Hardware, 6th Edition*.

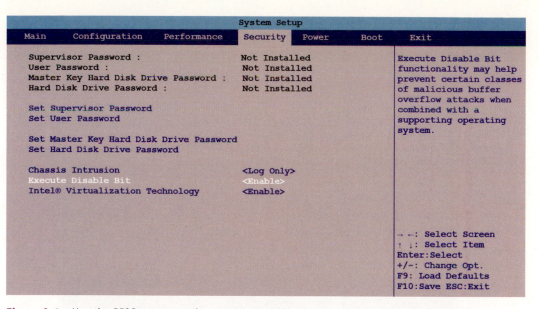

Figure 2-1 Use the BIOS setup security screen to enable the NX processor feature, which Intel calls Execute Disable Bit
Used with permission from Microsoft Corporation

SSE2 (STREAMING SIMD EXTENSIONS 2)

The **SSE2 (Streaming SIMD Extensions 2)** technology has been used by Intel and AMD processors since around 2001. SIMD stands for "single instruction, multiple data" and allows the processor to receive a single instruction and then execute it on multiple pieces of data as the data streams through. SSE2 has a larger instruction set than the original SSE, and SSE3 improves on SSE2. SSE4 increases the instruction set to improve 3D imaging for gaming and improves performance with data mining applications. The feature is always working and doesn't need to be enabled in BIOS setup.

WINDOWS 8 UPGRADE ASSISTANT

To verify that your computer hardware and applications qualify for Windows 8, you can run the Upgrade Assistant available on the Microsoft.com website. Here's how:

1. Go to **windows.microsoft.com/en-us/windows-8/upgrade-assistant-download-online-faq**. Click **Download Windows 8.1 Upgrade Assistant** or click **Download Windows 8 Upgrade Assistant**. The program files download. Click **Run** to respond to the Security Warning box, and then respond to the UAC box.

> 📝 **Notes** Websites change often. If you can't find the Upgrade Assistant at the link given, try this search string using google.com: **windows 8 upgrade assistant site:microsoft.com**.

2. The Upgrade Assistant launches, examines your system, and reports what it finds. A report for one system is shown in Figure 2-2. When you click **See compatibility details**, the Compatibility details box appears where you can save or print the report.

Before you upgrade to Windows 8, research each item that's not compatible, install an update if available, or uninstall the software or device. You can deal with most problems

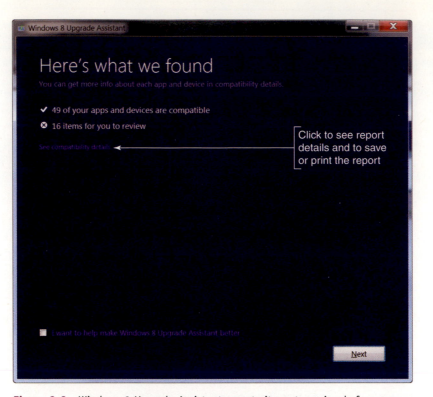

Figure 2-2   Windows 8 Upgrade Assistant reports items to review before you upgrade to Windows 8
Used with permission from Microsoft Corporation

after Windows 8 is installed, unless it's a critical device such as your network adapter. (You don't want to install Windows 8 only to find out later you can't access the network or Internet.)

EDITIONS OF WINDOWS 8

Microsoft has released Windows 8, Windows 8 Professional, and Windows 8 Enterprise for netbooks, notebooks, tablet PCs, and desktop computers. In addition, Windows RT is used on some smartphones, tablets, and low-end PCs. Here are the major differences among these editions of Windows 8:

- Windows RT comes preinstalled on tablets, tablet PCs, netbooks, and other mobile devices that use an ARM processor. Windows RT allows you to download apps from the Microsoft Store, but you can't install programs on the Windows desktop. It also supports BitLocker Encryption.
- Windows 8 replaces Windows 7 Starter, Windows 7 Home Basic, and Windows 7 Home Premium as the choice for a netbook, notebook, or desktop computer used in a home or small office. Windows 8 supports homegroups, but you can't use it to join a domain. It does not support BitLocker.
- Windows 8 Professional (Windows 8 Pro) replaces Windows 7 Professional and includes BitLocker, Client Hyper-V, and Group Policy and the ability to join a domain and host Remote Desktop. You can also boot a system from a virtual hard drive

(VHD) using Windows 8 Professional. You learn how to use Client Hyper-V later in the chapter.

▲ **Windows 8 Enterprise** allows for volume licensing in an enterprise and includes Windows to Go.

INSTALL WINDOWS 8 AS AN UPGRADE OR CLEAN INSTALL

An upgrade license of Windows 8 or Windows 8 Pro costs less than a license for a new installation. You can use this upgrade license on computers that already have Windows 7/Vista/XP installed. For Windows Vista or XP, you can use the upgrade license, but you must perform a clean install of Windows 8. Windows knows which type of license you've purchased by the product key when it's used to activate Windows 8.

In general, a 32-bit installation of Windows 7 can be upgraded to a 32-bit installation of Windows 8. A 64-bit installation of Windows 7 can be upgraded to a 64-bit installation of Windows 8. If you want to install a 64-bit installation of Windows 8 on a system that currently has a 32-bit OS installed, you must do a clean install.

If your system is giving errors or is especially sluggish, it's probably best to get a fresh start by performing a clean install. On the other hand, an in-place upgrade works well on a healthy system because it's faster—you don't need to reinstall the applications, and data and user settings stay intact.

> 📝 **Notes** The steps and screenshots for an in-place upgrade in this section are for Windows 8.1. The steps for Windows 8 work about the same way.

STEPS TO PERFORM A WINDOWS 8 IN-PLACE UPGRADE

The Windows 8 and Windows 8.1 retail packages come with a 32-bit DVD and a 64-bit DVD (see Figure 2-3). The product key is on a card found in a slip pocket inside the box. You can perform an in-place upgrade from Windows 7 to Windows 8 or from Windows 8 to Windows 8.1. You cannot perform an in-place upgrade from Windows 7 directly to Windows 8.1. For this situation, you can upgrade Windows 7 to Windows 8 and then upgrade to Windows 8.1.

Figure 2-3 Windows 8 and Windows 8.1 packages come with two DVDs and one product key
Copyright © 2015 Cengage Learning

Here are the steps to perform an in-place upgrade from Windows 7 to Windows 8 or from Windows 8 to Windows 8.1 when you're working with a Windows 8 or 8.1 setup DVD:

1. As with any upgrade installation, before you start the upgrade, do the following:

   a. Scan the system for malware using an updated version of antivirus software. When you're done, be sure to close the antivirus application so it's not running in the background.

   b. Uninstall any applications or device drivers you don't intend to use in the new installation.

   c. Make sure your backups of important data are up to date, and then close any backup software running in the background.

> **? To Learn More** To learn more about what to do before you upgrade Windows, start at page 274 in Chapter 7 of *A+ Guide to Managing and Maintaining Your PC, 8th Edition*, or page 38 of Chapter 2 in *A+ Guide to Software, 6th Edition*.

2. Insert the Windows 8 setup DVD. If the setup program doesn't start automatically and the AutoPlay dialog box doesn't open, open Windows Explorer and double-click the setup program in the root of the DVD. Respond to the UAC box. The setup program loads files, examines the system, and reports any problems it finds. If it finds the system meets minimum hardware requirements, setup asks permission to go online for updates (see Figure 2-4). Make your selection, and click **Next**.

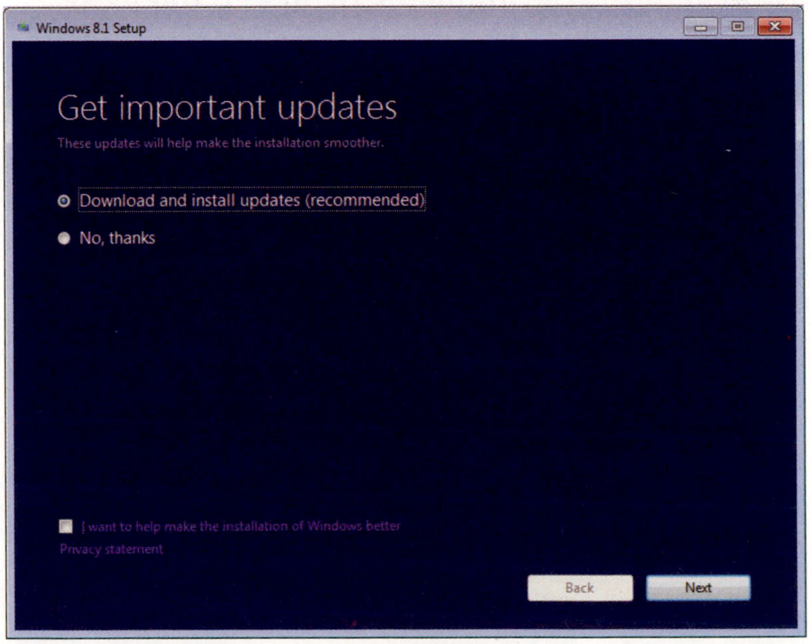

Figure 2-4   Decide how you will handle updates to the setup process
Used with permission from Microsoft Corporation

3. The next window requests the product key (see Figure 2-5). Enter the product key, and Windows verifies the key is a valid key. Click **Next**.

4. The License terms window appears. Check **I accept the license terms**, and click **Accept**.

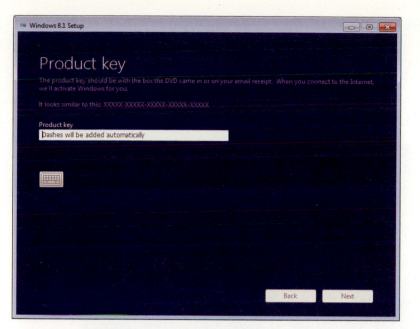

Figure 2-5 The product key is verified as a valid key before you can continue with the installation
Used with permission from Microsoft Corporation

Figure 2-6 Decide what to keep of the old installation
Used with permission from Microsoft Corporation

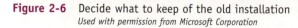

5. On the *Choose what to keep* screen (see Figure 2-6), decide what you want to do with Windows settings, personal files, and apps:

   ◢ The first option performs an upgrade to Windows 8 or 8.1.
   ◢ The last two options perform a clean install of Windows 8 or 8.1. When you choose the Nothing option, drive C is formatted, but other volumes on the hard drive are not disturbed.

   For an upgrade installation, choose the first option, and click **Next**. On the next screen, verify the choices listed, and click **Install** to begin the installation.

📋 **Notes** When setup recognizes that it cannot perform an upgrade, but must perform a clean install, the first option on the screen in Figure 2-6 is missing, for example, when you attempt to upgrade from Windows 7 directly to Windows 8.1.

---

6. During the installation, setup might restart the system several times. Near the end of the installation, you are asked to select a screen color (see Figure 2-7).

Figure 2-7 Select a screen color
Used with permission from Microsoft Corporation

7. Next, the Settings screen appears (see Figure 2-8). To use the settings listed, click **Use express settings**. To customize the settings, click **Customize**, and make your selections for these settings:

   ▲ Settings for sharing and connecting to devices
   ▲ Automatic Windows updates
   ▲ Privacy settings for apps and Internet Explorer
   ▲ Information sent to Microsoft

8. If the computer is connected to the Internet, on the next screen, you are given the opportunity to enter a Microsoft account that you can use to sign in to Windows (see Figure 2-9). Recall from Chapter 1 that a Microsoft account is associated with an email address registered at live.com.

   You have three options for signing in to Windows 8:

   ▲ To use an existing Microsoft account, enter the email address and password, and click **Next**.
   ▲ If you want to create a new Microsoft account, click **Create a new account**. On the next screen that appears (see Figure 2-10), enter the information for the new account, and click **Next**. Notice on the screen you can get a new Microsoft email address (outlook.com, hotmail.com, or live.com address), or you can use an existing email address (one that is not managed by Microsoft).
   ▲ If you want to continue using your local account, on the screen shown in Figure 2-9, click **Create a new account**. On the next screen (see Figure 2-10), click **Continue using my existing account**. (You can switch to a Microsoft account later, after Windows 8 is installed.)

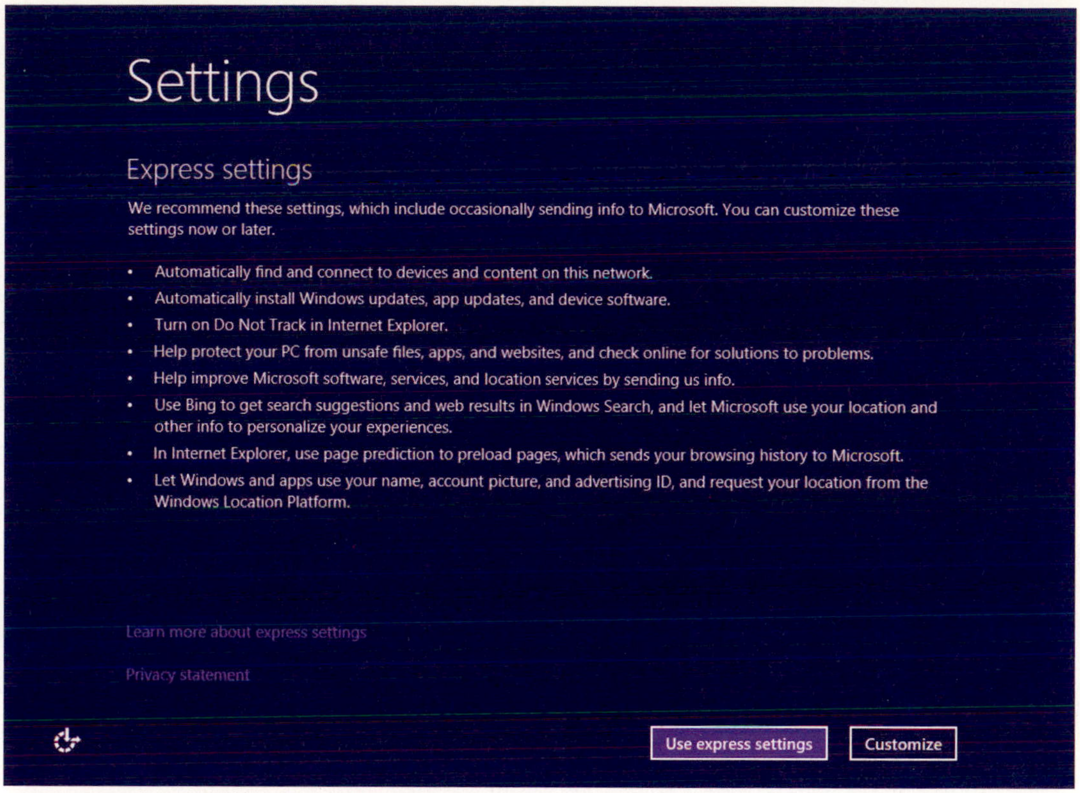

Settings

Express settings

We recommend these settings, which include occasionally sending info to Microsoft. You can customize these settings now or later.

- Automatically find and connect to devices and content on this network.
- Automatically install Windows updates, app updates, and device software.
- Turn on Do Not Track in Internet Explorer.
- Help protect your PC from unsafe files, apps, and websites, and check online for solutions to problems.
- Help improve Microsoft software, services, and location services by sending us info.
- Use Bing to get search suggestions and web results in Windows Search, and let Microsoft use your location and other info to personalize your experiences.
- In Internet Explorer, use page prediction to preload pages, which sends your browsing history to Microsoft.
- Let Windows and apps use your name, account picture, and advertising ID, and request your location from the Windows Location Platform.

Learn more about express settings

Privacy statement

[Use express settings] [Customize]

Figure 2-8 Decide which settings to accept
Used with permission from Microsoft Corporation

← Sign in to your Microsoft account

Sign in to easily get your online email, photos, files, and settings (like browser history and favorites) on all your devices. You can manage your synced settings at any time.

⎡ Sign in using an
⎢ existing Microsoft
⎣ account

Password

Don't have an account?
Create a new account ←

⎡ Sign up for a new Microsoft account,
⎢ and use it to sign in to Windows 8
⎢ or sign in using your existing local
⎣ account

Privacy statement

[Next]

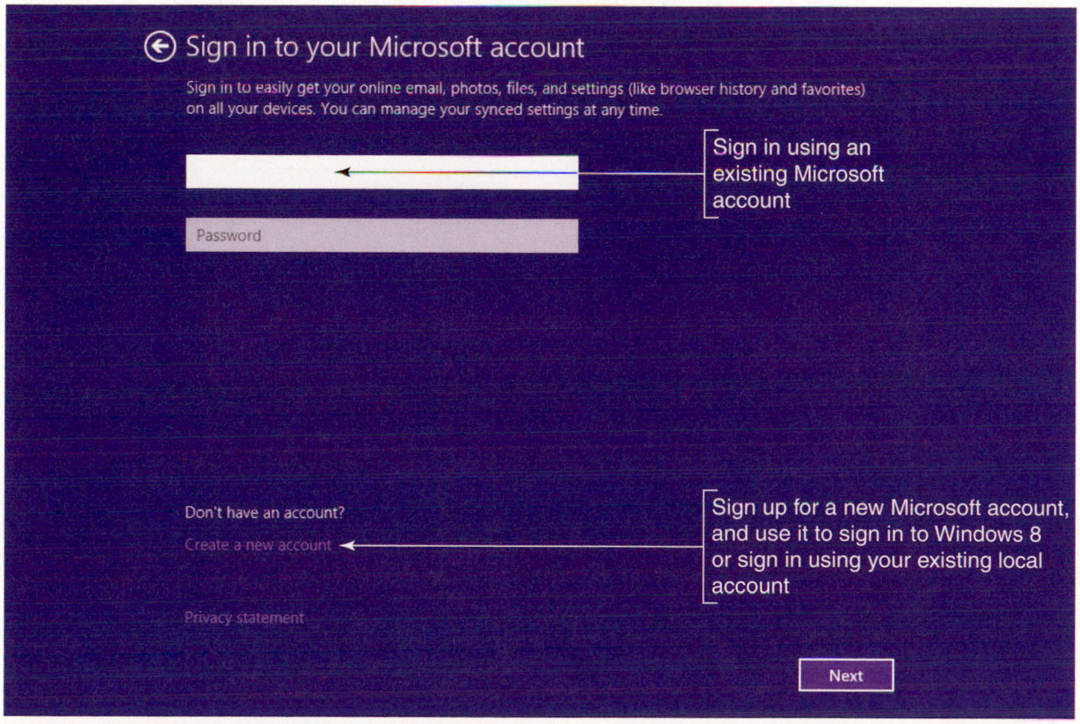

Figure 2-9 Decide which account you will use to sign in to Windows 8
Used with permission from Microsoft Corporation

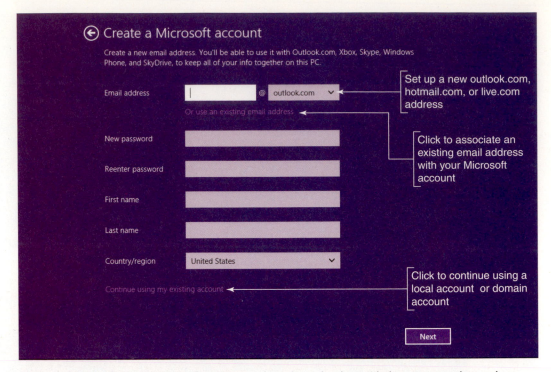

Figure 2-10   Create a new Microsoft account and use it to sign in to Windows 8 or continue using a
local or domain account
Used with permission from Microsoft Corporation

9. If you're signing in with a Microsoft account, follow directions on screen to set up how you want to secure your Microsoft account on this computer and set up your SkyDrive.

10. Settings are applied, and the Windows Start screen appears. You can now use the new installation of Windows 8.

📝 Notes   When you first start using Windows 8.1 after an installation, it provides tips on screen to help you learn to use the OS (see Figure 2-11). The only way to get rid of a tip on screen is to follow its directions.

You just saw how to perform an upgrade using the Windows setup DVD. You can also download from the Microsoft website the files you need to perform the upgrade. To do that, Microsoft requires you first run the Upgrade Assistant. Here's how to get started:

1. After you have your Windows computer ready to upgrade, go to **windows.microsoft.com/en-us/windows-8/upgrade-to-windows-8**. Click **Download Upgrade Assistant**. Run the **Windows 8 Upgrade Assistant**. Make sure you have Windows 8 device drivers already downloaded for such critical devices as your network adapter.

2. If you're ready to proceed with the upgrade, click **Next** to continue.

3. The *Choose what to keep* window appears (refer back to Figure 2-6). Make your choice, and click **Next**.

4. On the next screen, Microsoft recommends the right edition of Windows (see Figure 2-12). To buy the edition, click **Order**. On the next screen, click **Checkout**.

2

Figure 2-11 Tip boxes appear on Windows 8.1 screens to help you learn to use the OS
Used with permission from Microsoft Corporation

Figure 2-12 Microsoft offers Windows 8 Pro for purchase
Used with permission from Microsoft Corporation

5. Follow directions on screen to enter your name, phone number, email address, and billing address, then pay for and start the download.

6. After the download completes, the Install Windows 8 screen appears. You can click *Install now* to continue with the installation. If you click *Install by creating media*, you are given the opportunity to create a bootable USB flash drive or DVD that contains the Windows setup files. You're also given the opportunity to save the setup files to an ISO file. Later, you can use the USB flash drive or DVD to perform the upgrade to Windows 8. As you'll see later in the chapter, the ISO file is a handy tool when you want to install Windows in a virtual machine.

STEPS TO PERFORM A WINDOWS 8 CLEAN INSTALL

Recall that a clean install is the best option to use if the current installation is sluggish or giving problems or if you're installing Windows 8 on a new desktop computer you're building.

If you have a Windows 7/Vista/XP installation that qualifies for a Windows 8 upgrade, and you need to do a clean install, begin by starting the installation from the Windows desktop as you would for an upgrade. When you get to the window shown earlier in Figure 2-6, click **Nothing**, and continue with the installation. The volume holding the old Windows installation is formatted, and everything on the volume is lost. If the hard drive has other volumes, these volumes are left unchanged.

> **Notes** The steps and screenshots for a clean install in this section are for Windows 8.1. The steps for Windows 8 work about the same way.

Here are the steps to perform a clean install on a new hard drive using a product key purchased for a new installation of Windows 8.1:

1. Boot from the Windows setup DVD or USB flash drive. In the Windows Setup screen (see Figure 2-13), select the language and other preferences, and click **Next**. On the next screen, click **Install now**.

Figure 2-13 Decide on language and keyboard preferences
Used with permission from Microsoft Corporation

2. Enter your product key on the next screen. Setup verifies the key is a valid product key. (It doesn't verify that the key is approved for a clean install. That happens when you attempt to activate Windows.) Click **Next**.

3. Accept the license agreement on the next screen, and click **Next**. On the next screen (see Figure 2-14), click **Custom: Install Windows only (advanced)**.

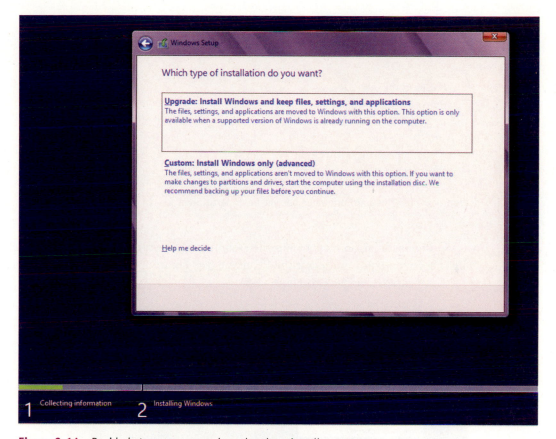

Figure 2-14   Decide between an upgrade and a clean install
Used with permission from Microsoft Corporation

4. The *Where do you want to install Windows?* screen appears. Select the drive and volume where you want to install Windows. Figure 2-15 shows the screen that appears for a new hard drive that has not been partitioned. By default, setup will use the entire unallocated space for the Windows volume. If you want to use only a portion of the space, click **New** and enter the size of the volume. (Setup will also create a small reserved partition that it later uses for system files and the startup process.) Click **Next** to continue.

> **Notes** If you don't see the *New* link on the *Where do you want to install Windows?* screen, click *Drive options (advanced)* to see this and other links you can use to manage the space on the hard drive.

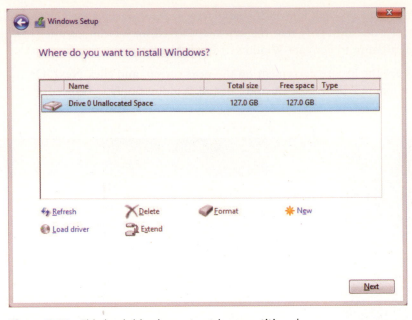

Figure 2-15 This hard drive has not yet been partitioned
Used with permission from Microsoft Corporation

5. The installation begins, and the system might restart several times. You can then select a screen color and enter the PC name (see Figure 2-16). Next, the Settings screen appears (refer back to Figure 2-8).

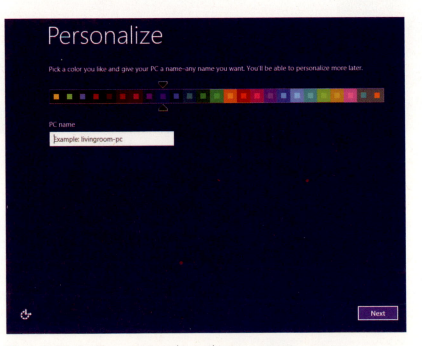

Figure 2-16 Decide on screen color, and enter a computer name
Used with permission from Microsoft Corporation

6. After you have made your choices on the Settings screen, the *Sign in to your Microsoft account* screen appears where you can set up a Microsoft account for this system (shown earlier in Figure 2-9). You have three options:

▲ To use an existing email address, enter the email address, and click **Next**. Windows checks to see if it is not already associated with a Microsoft account. If it is not, you will be asked to enter the information needed to create the account.

◢ If you want to create a new email address to be associated with a new Microsoft account, click **Create a new account**. On the *Create a Microsoft account* screen that appears (see Figure 2-17), enter the information for the new account, and click **Next**.

◢ If you want to use a local account, on the screen shown in Figure 2-17, click **Sign in without a Microsoft account**. The screen shown in Figure 2-18 appears. Enter the local account name, password, and password hint, and click **Finish**.

7. The installation continues, settings are applied, and the Start screen appears. You can now use the new installation of Windows 8.

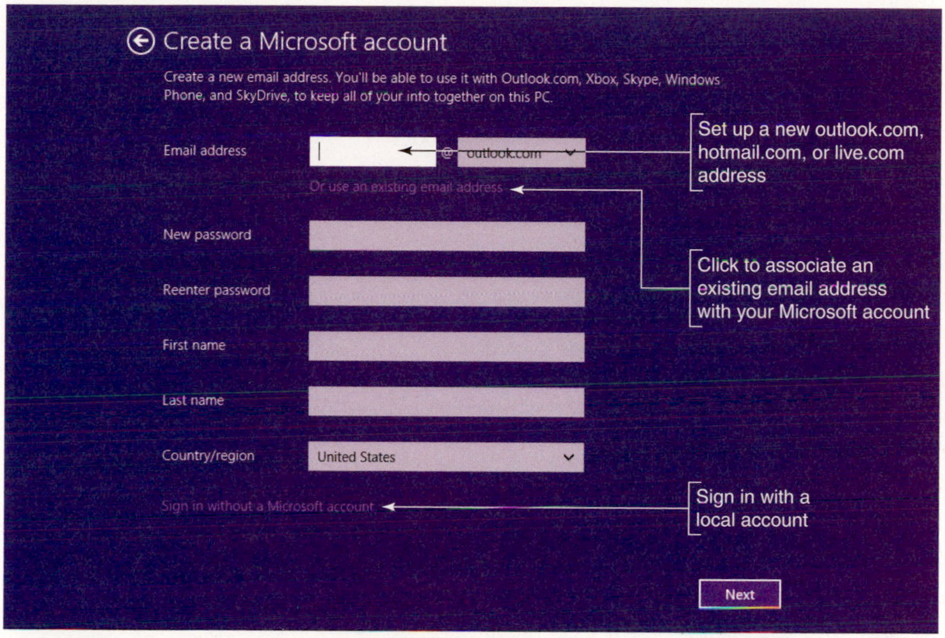

2

⊖ Create a Microsoft account

Create a new email address. You'll be able to use it with Outlook.com, Xbox, Skype, Windows Phone, and SkyDrive, to keep all of your info together on this PC.

| Email address | | @ outlook.com ▾ | |

Or use an existing email address

Set up a new outlook.com, hotmail.com, or live.com address

| New password | | |
| Reenter password | | |

Click to associate an existing email address with your Microsoft account

First name		
Last name		
Country/region	United States ▾	

Sign in without a Microsoft account ←

Sign in with a local account

Next

Figure 2-17 Decide how you will sign in to Windows
Used with permission from Microsoft Corporation

⊖ Your account

If you want a password, choose something that will be easy for you to remember but hard for others to guess.

User name	Example: John
Password	
Reenter password	
Password hint	

Finish

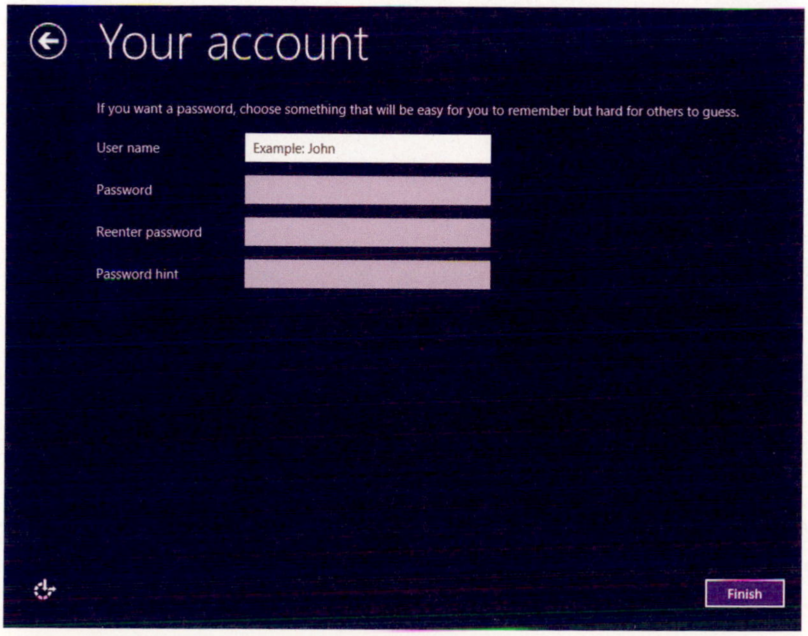

Figure 2-18 Set up a local account
Used with permission from Microsoft Corporation

STEPS TO SET UP A WINDOWS 8 DUAL BOOT

To set up a dual boot system with another operating system (such as Windows 7), follow these steps:

1. Each OS must be installed in its own partition. Make sure you have enough free space on a partition that doesn't currently hold an OS. Or, you can use unallocated space on the drive to create a new partition while installing Windows 8. Recall that Windows 8 needs about 16 GB or 20 GB free space.

2. Start the installation by booting from the Windows setup DVD or USB flash drive. The Windows Setup screen shown earlier in Figure 2-13 appears. Make your selections, and click **Next**. On the next screen, click **Install now**.

3. On the next screen, enter your product key, and click **Next**. On the next screen, accept the license agreement, and click **Next**.

4. On the next screen (refer back to Figure 2-14), click **Custom: Install Windows only (advanced)**.

5. On the next screen, select the partition or unallocated space to hold the installation. For example, select **Unallocated Space** to hold the Windows 8 installation, as shown in Figure 2-19. Don't select the partition where the older operating system is already installed; doing so causes setup to install Windows 8 in place of the older OS. Click **Next**. The installation continues as it does for a clean install.

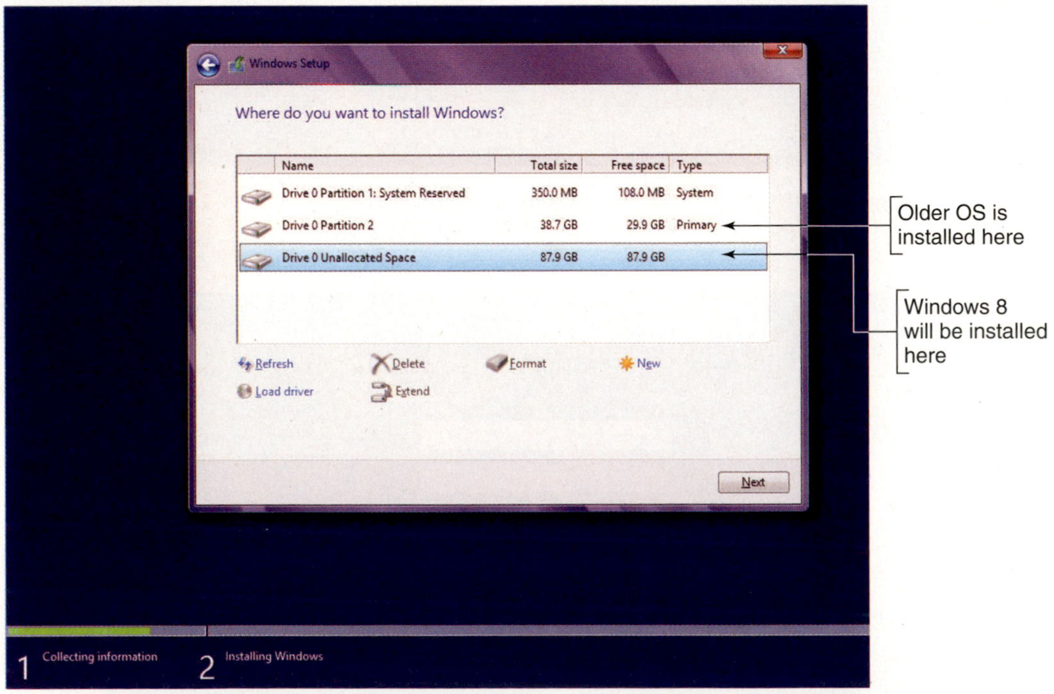

Figure 2-19   Select unallocated space or a partition other than the one used by the first OS installation
Used with permission from Microsoft Corporation

HOW TO USE AN UPGRADE PRODUCT KEY FOR A CLEAN INSTALL ON A NEW HARD DRIVE

Suppose you want to use a Windows 8 upgrade product key for an installation on a new hard drive. This might be the case if you've just replaced a failed hard drive that was using the product key. Here's how to perform a clean install of Windows 8 using an upgrade product key:

1. Boot from the Windows 8 upgrade DVD or USB flash drive and install Windows 8 as a clean install. When you enter the product key, know that setup verifies only that the key is a valid key; it doesn't verify that the key works for a clean install. However, you won't be able to activate Windows 8 using this product key with a clean install unless you call Microsoft and explain the situation.

2. Boot into Windows and install Windows 8 a second time, this time as an upgrade. The product key is accepted by setup as a valid product key, and you should later have no problems activating Windows 8 without assistance from Microsoft.

WHAT TO DO AFTER THE INSTALLATION

As with any Windows installation, after the OS is installed, you need to

- Verify you have network access
- Activate Windows
- Install updates for Windows (including Windows 8.1 if it's not already installed)
- Verify automatic update settings are as you want them
- Install hardware and applications
- Set up user accounts, and transfer or restore from backup user data and preferences
- Turn Windows features on or off
- For a mobile computer, verify power management settings. (To open the Power Options window, press **Win+X**, and click **Power Options**.)

Next, let's look at how to do the tasks that differ significantly in Windows 8 from those in Windows 7.

VERIFY NETWORK ACCESS AND SECURITY SETTINGS

To make a wired connection to a network, simply plug in the network cable and Windows does the rest. To create a wireless connection, follow these steps:

1. On the charms bar, click the **Settings** charm, and then click the network icon. A list of available wireless networks appears (see Figure 2-20a). Click one to select it, and then click **Connect** (see Figure 2-20b).

2. If the network is secured, you must enter the security key to connect.

Windows 8 offers two basic types of network security: Public and Private. When using Public network security, you cannot join a homegroup or domain, and Windows configures strong firewall settings. Using Private network security, you can join a homegroup or domain and share files and printers. (A Private network is similar to a Work or Home network location in Windows 7, and a Public network is similar to a Public network location in Windows 7.)

To view and change network security settings, click the **Settings** charm and click **Change PC settings**. On the PC settings screen, click **Network**. On the Network screen, if necessary, click **Connections** (see Figure 2-21).

> **Notes** When you click **HomeGroup** on the Network screen shown in Figure 2-21, you can use the HomeGroup page that appears to join or leave a homegroup, view the homegroup password, and decide whether libraries and printers are shared with the homegroup. These homegroup settings can also be managed from the Network and Sharing Center.

(a)   (b)

Figure 2-20   (a) View a list of available wireless networks, and (b) select a
wireless network to connect
Used with permission from Microsoft Corporation

Figure 2-21   Use the Network screen to manage the security of network
connections
Used with permission from Microsoft Corporation

When you click a connection in the right pane, you can view and change some of
the properties for the connection. For example, Figure 2-22 shows a wired connection
and Figure 2-23 shows a wireless connection. To set the network security to Private,
turn on **Find devices and content**. To set the network security to Public, turn this
setting off.

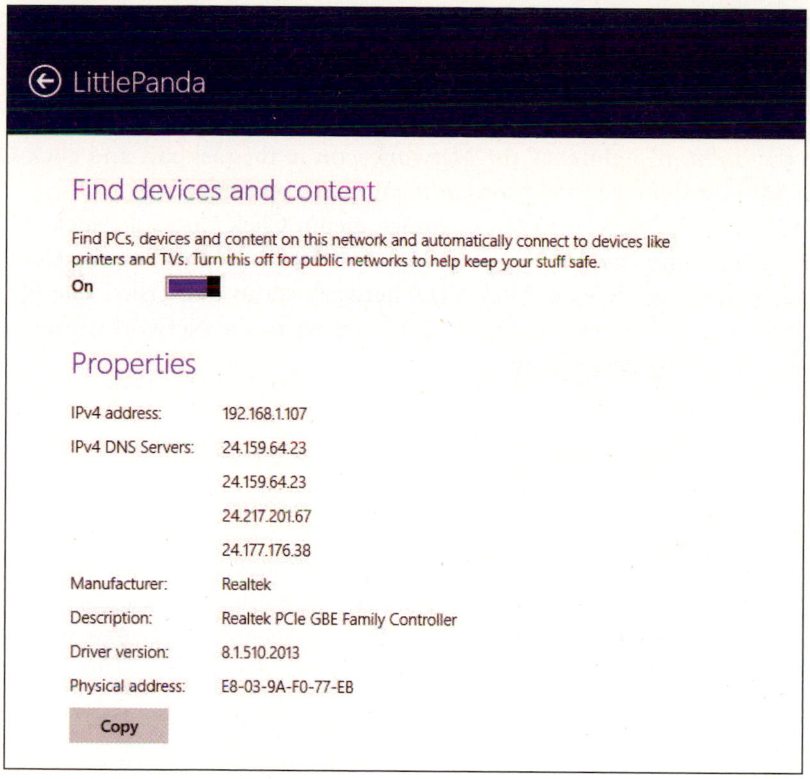

2

← LittlePanda

Find devices and content

Find PCs, devices and content on this network and automatically connect to devices like printers and TVs. Turn this off for public networks to help keep your stuff safe.

On   [On]

Properties

IPv4 address:	192.168.1.107
IPv4 DNS Servers:	24.159.64.23
	24.159.64.23
	24.217.201.67
	24.177.176.38
Manufacturer:	Realtek
Description:	Realtek PCIe GBE Family Controller
Driver version:	8.1.510.2013
Physical address:	E8-03-9A-F0-77-EB

Copy

Figure 2-22   View and manage a wired network connection
Used with permission from Microsoft Corporation

← LittlePanda

Find devices and content

Find PCs, devices and content on this network and automatically connect to devices like printers and TVs. Turn this off for public networks to help keep your stuff safe.

On   [On]

Data usage

Show my estimated data use in the Networks list

Off   [Off]

Set as a metered connection

Off   [Off]

Properties

SSID:	LittlePanda
Protocol:	802.11n
Security type:	WPA2-Personal
IPv4 address:	192.168.1.132
IPv4 DNS Servers:	24.159.64.23
	24.159.64.23

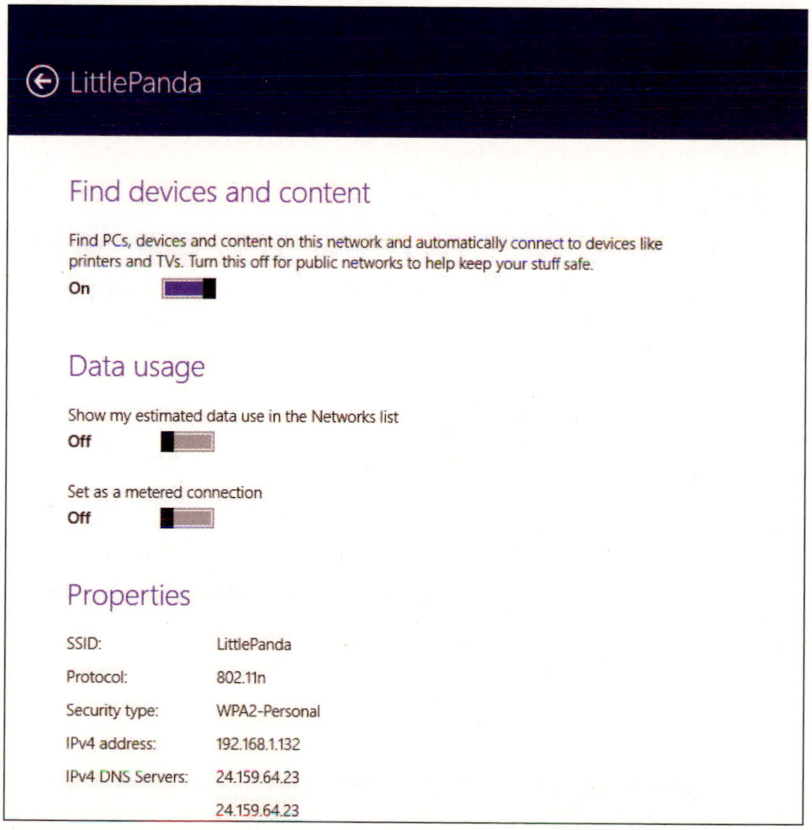

Figure 2-23   View and manage a wireless network connection
Used with permission from Microsoft Corporation

For more advanced control of security and to troubleshoot network problems, use the Network and Sharing Center. To open the Network and Sharing Center, use one of these methods:

▲ On the desktop, right-click the **Network** icon in the taskbar, and click **Open Network and Sharing Center** in the shortcut menu that appears.

▲ Press **Win+X** to open the Quick Launch menu. Click **Control Panel**. When Control Panel is in icon view (see Figure 2-24), click **Network and Sharing Center**. If Control Panel is in Category view, click **View network status and tasks**. The Network and Sharing Center is shown in Figure 2-25. To get to the Network Connections window, click **Change adapter settings**.

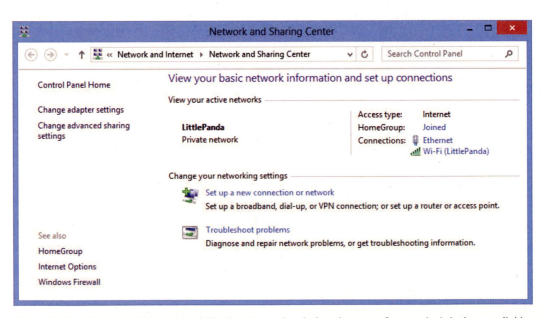

Figure 2-24   Windows 8 Control Panel in Small icons view
Used with permission from Microsoft Corporation

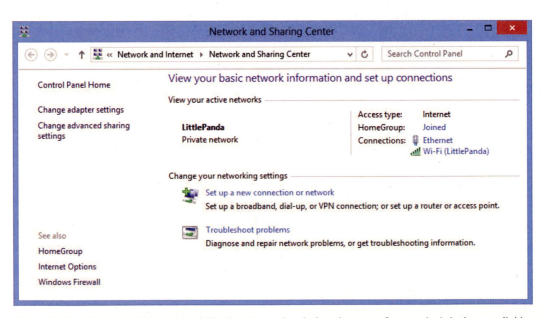

Figure 2-25   Windows 8 Network and Sharing Center is missing the map of networked devices available in Windows 7
Used with permission from Microsoft Corporation

◢ For a shortcut to the Network Connections window, press **Win+X**, and click **Network Connections** in the Quick Launch menu. The Network Connections window is shown in Figure 2-26.

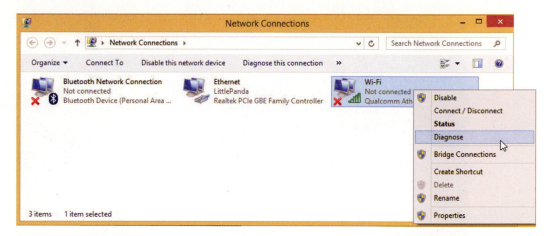

Figure 2-26 Use the Network Connections window to troubleshoot a wired or wireless network connection
Used with permission from Microsoft Corporation

In the Network Connections window, a quick way to repair a connection is to right-click a connection and use the shortcut menu as shown in Figure 2-26. Click **Diagnose** or **Connect/Disconnect** to have Windows repair the connection. You can also disable and then enable the connection to reset the network adapter.

In addition, Table 2-1 lists some other tasks when managing wireless networks. Some require an elevated command prompt window. To open the window, go to the Apps screen, and right-click **Command Prompt**. In the status bar at the bottom of the screen, click **Run as administrator** (see Figure 2-27), and respond to the UAC box. The command prompt window appears.

Task	Directions
To view a list of networks the computer has connected to:	In a command prompt window, use this command (see Figure 2-28): `netsh wlan show profiles`
For a network you're connected to, to show its security key:	In the Network and Sharing Center, click *Change adapter settings*. Right-click the network, and click *Status*. In the Status box, click *Wireless Properties*. In the Properties box, click the *Security* tab, and check *Show characters*.
For any network you have previously connected to, to show its security key:	In a command prompt window, use this command: `netsh wlan show profile name="profile name" key=clear`
To delete a network profile:	In a command prompt window, use this command: `netsh wlan delete profile name= "profile name"`

Table 2-1 Tasks for managing wireless networks

Copyright © 2015 Cengage Learning

Notes To open a normal command prompt window, press **Win+X**, and click **Run**. In the Run dialog box, type **cmd**, and press **Enter**. Or, start typing **command** on the Start screen, and then click **Command Prompt**.

Click to open an
elevated command
prompt window

Figure 2-27 Use the status bar to open an elevated command prompt window
Used with permission from Microsoft Corporation

Figure 2-28 Use an elevated command prompt window and advanced tools to manage wireless networks
Used with permission from Microsoft Corporation

Managing advanced sharing options for folders, files, and printers on the network works
about the same as it does in Windows 7. For example, to manage sharing settings, go to the
Network and Sharing Center, and click **Change advanced sharing settings** in the left pane.
The Advanced sharing settings window appears where you can change sharing options
(see Figure 2-29). To set sharing options for individual folders and files, open the **Properties**
box for a folder or file, and change sharing options on the Sharing tab and Security tab as
you do in Windows 7.

? To Learn More To learn more about advanced sharing for files and folders, start at page 835 in Chapter 17 of *A+ Guide to Managing and Maintaining Your PC, 8th Edition*, or page 383 in Chapter 8 of *A+ Guide to Software, 6th Edition*.

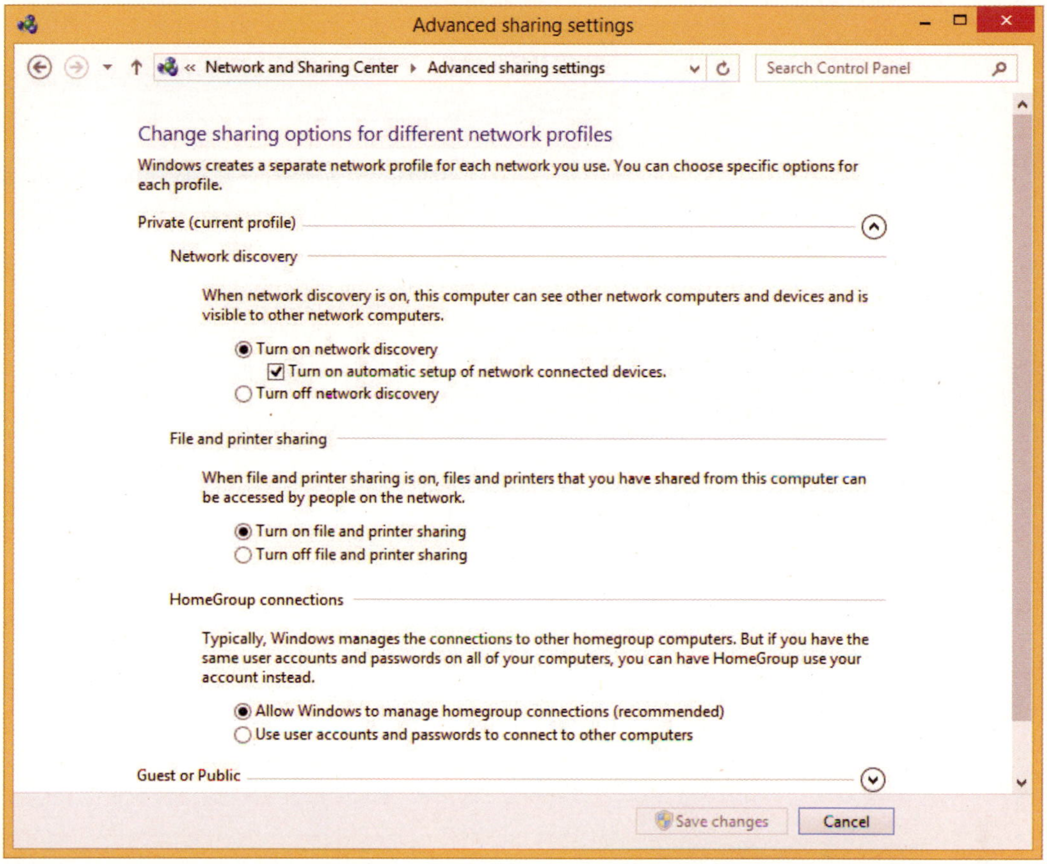

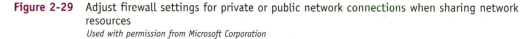

Figure 2-29 Adjust firewall settings for private or public network connections when sharing network resources
Used with permission from Microsoft Corporation

If you need additional control over firewall settings, in the Network and Sharing Center, click **Windows Firewall**. The Windows Firewall window opens (see the top-left window in Figure 2-30). The window works similar to that in Windows 7. For even more details, click **Advanced settings**. The Windows Firewall with Advanced Security window opens (see the bottom-right window in Figure 2-30). For example, to set many firewall details about an app that uses the Internet, click Inbound Rules or Outbound Rules in the left pane, select the app in the middle pane, and click **Properties** in the right pane.

? To Learn More To learn more about Windows Firewall settings, start at page 885 in Chapter 18 of *A+ Guide to Managing and Maintaining Your PC, 8th Edition*, or page 433 in Chapter 9 of *A+ Guide to Software, 6th Edition*.

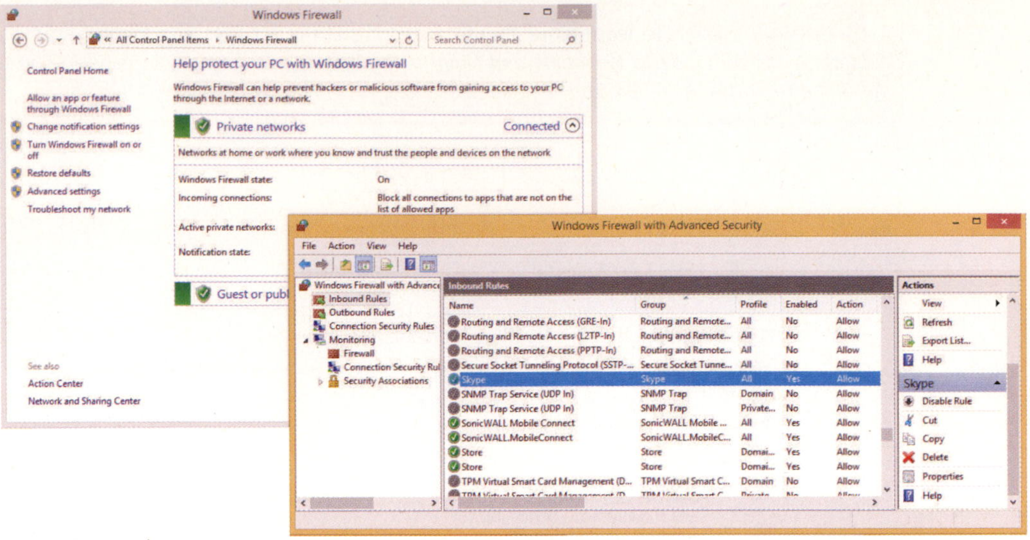

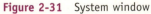

Figure 2-30 Use the advanced security settings in Windows Firewall to control how an app can use the network for inbound or outbound traffic
Used with permission from Microsoft Corporation

ACTIVATE WINDOWS 8

Windows 8 setup requires you to enter a product key during the installation, and, if the computer is connected to the Internet, Windows will automatically activate. To view the product key and the activation status, go to the System window. Figure 2-31 shows the window for one system that is not activated. To activate, make sure you're connected to the Internet, and click **Activate Windows**.

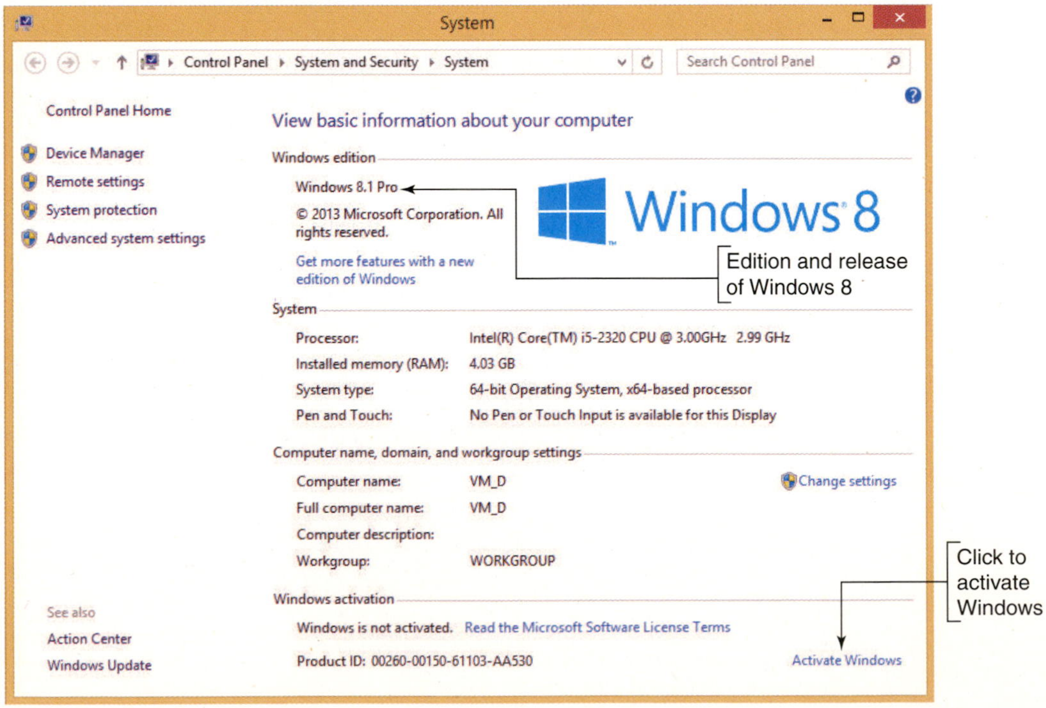

Figure 2-31 System window
Used with permission from Microsoft Corporation

> **Notes** One way to open the System window is to press **Win+X**, and click **System**. You can also type **system** on the Start screen, and then click **System**. By the way, notice the System window is missing the Windows Experience Index that was available in earlier Windows editions.

MANAGE WINDOWS UPDATES

To view and manage Windows update settings, open the **System** window, and click **Windows Update** in the left pane (refer back to Figure 2-31). In the Windows Update window (see Figure 2-32), you can view updates and install them. Before you move on, make sure all important updates are installed. To check for new updates, click **Check for updates** in the left pane. Keep installing important updates and checking for more updates until no more updates are available. You might need to restart the system after certain updates are installed.

Figure 2-32 View and manage Windows updates
Used with permission from Microsoft Corporation

Next, you need to make sure the update settings are as you want them. Click **Change settings**. In the Change settings window (see Figure 2-33), you can decide when and how updates are installed. Windows 8 automatically installs updates daily at 3:00 AM. (Windows 8.1 installs at 2:00 AM.) To change how updates are installed and the time installed or to decide whether Windows can wake up your computer to perform updates, click **Updates will be automatically installed during the maintenance window**.

UPGRADE TO WINDOWS 8.1

Here are the options to upgrade to Windows 8.1:

- ◢ After Windows 8 is installed, you can download the Windows 8.1 update free using the Windows Store app on the Start screen. Using this method, a product key is not requested.
- ◢ You can upgrade Windows 8 to Windows 8.1 using a Windows 8.1 setup DVD. Using this method, a product key is required.
- ◢ To upgrade Windows 7 to Windows 8.1, you must first upgrade to Windows 8 and then use the Windows Store to get the free Windows 8.1 update.

To find out which release of Windows is installed, press **Win+X**, and click **System**. The System window reports the release (look back at Figure 2-31).

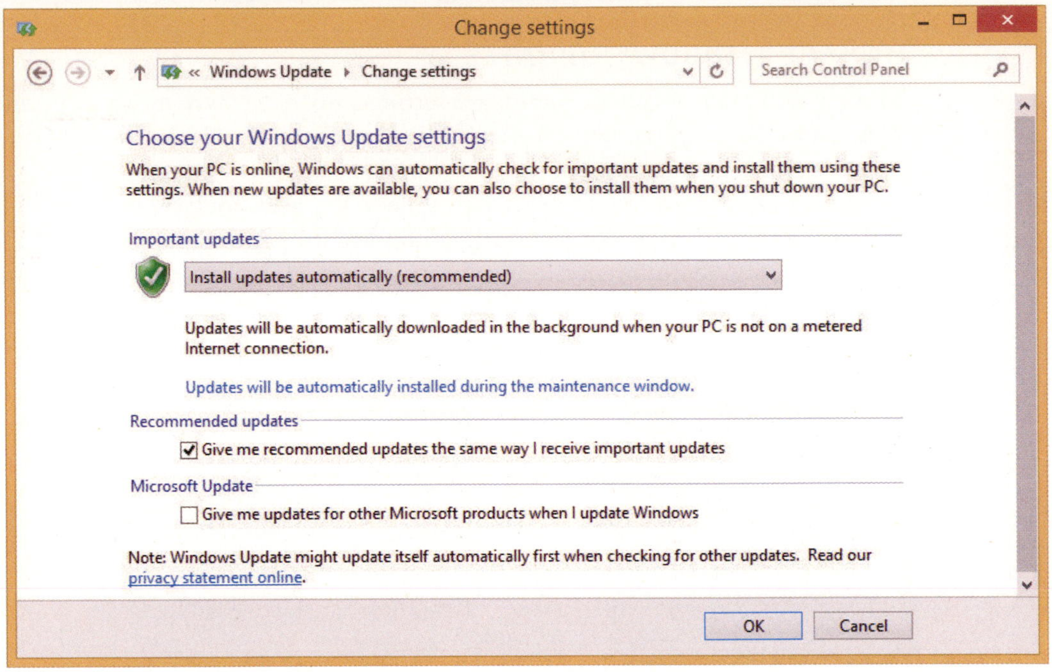

Figure 2-33   Decide how and when updates are installed
Used with permission from Microsoft Corporation

If you already have Windows 8 installed, you can get the Windows 8.1 upgrade free. Follow these steps:

1. In Windows 8, use the **System** window to check for updates and verify all important updates are installed. If the KB2871389 update is not installed, the Windows 8.1 update does not appear in the Windows Store.

2. Go to the **Start** screen, and open the **Store** app. Find and download the Windows 8.1 app. (If you don't see it, go back and make sure all Windows updates are applied and restart the system.) The process of installing Windows 8.1 is similar to installing Windows 8 as an upgrade. You must restart Windows, accept the license agreement, decide how Settings are handled, and set up a user account or use an existing account. Entering a product key is not required.

INSTALL AND UNINSTALL HARDWARE AND APPLICATIONS

Hardware and desktop applications are installed as they are in Windows 7. To install apps in the Windows 8 interface, use the Store app on the Start screen. To get to Device Manager to manage your device drivers and uninstall hardware, press **Win+X**, and click **Device Manager**. To uninstall desktop applications, press **Win+X**, and click **Programs and Features** in the Quick Launch menu that appears. In the Programs and Features window (see Figure 2-34), select an application, and then click **Uninstall** in the menu bar.

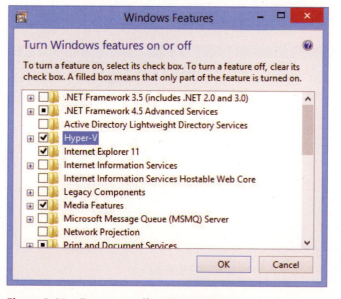

Figure 2-34 Uninstall, change, or repair desktop applications
Used with permission from Microsoft Corporation

Recall from Chapter 1 that you can uninstall a Windows 8 app by using the Start screen or Apps screen. Right-click the app tile, and then click **Uninstall** in the status bar that appears at the bottom of the screen.

TURN ON AND OFF WINDOWS FEATURES

To turn Windows features on or off, click **Turn Windows features on or off** in the Programs and Features window shown earlier in Figure 2-34. In the Windows Features window that appears (see Figure 2-35), check or uncheck a feature, and click **OK**. Sometimes a restart is necessary for the changes to take effect.

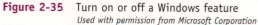

Figure 2-35 Turn on or off a Windows feature
Used with permission from Microsoft Corporation

INSTALLING AND USING VIRTUAL MACHINES WITH CLIENT HYPER-V

Client Hyper-V is the virtual machine (VM) manager that is part of 64-bit Windows 8 Pro. If your processor and motherboard support hardware-assisted virtualization (HAV), you can use Client Hyper-V to install and manage virtual machines on the desktop. Generation 1 VMs allow either a 32-bit or 64-bit installation of an OS in a VM. Generation 2 VMs require a 64-bit guest operating system. Hyper-V connects a VM to the local network by the way of a **virtual switch** that you must set up and connect to the physical network. Client Hyper-V supports dynamically expanding virtual hard drives and dynamically allocated memory. When using **dynamic memory**, the VM ties up only the portion of allocated memory that it is actually using.

> **Notes** Generation 2 used for VMs in Client Hyper-V became available with Windows 8.1.

APPLYING CONCEPTS

SETTING UP A VM

Here are the steps to set up a VM using Windows 8 Pro:

1. Go into BIOS setup on your computer, and make sure virtualization is enabled.

> **? To Learn More** To learn more about hardware-assisted virtualization and how to enable it, start at page 1,041 of Chapter 20 in *A+ Guide to Managing and Maintaining Your PC, 8th Edition*, and page 523 of Chapter 10 in *A+ Guide to Software, 6th Edition*.

2. Hyper-V is disabled in Windows 8 Pro by default. To turn it on, use the Windows Features window as shown earlier in Figure 2-35. You'll need to restart the system for the change to take effect.

3. To launch the Hyper-V Manager, go to the **Start** screen, and start typing **Hyper-V**, and then click **Hyper-V Manager**. Alternately, you can click the Hyper-V Manager tile on the Start screen. The Hyper-V Manager window appears on the desktop. In the Hyper-V Manager pane on the left, select the host computer (see Figure 2-36).

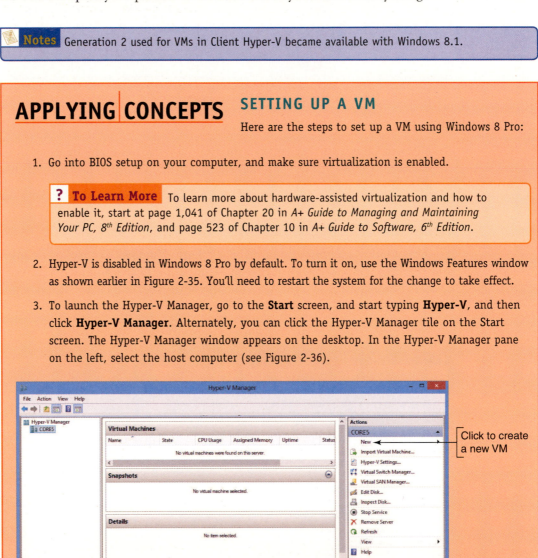

Figure 2-36 The host computer is selected for managing Hyper-V virtual machines
Used with permission from Microsoft Corporation

4. If you want your VMs to have access to the network or the Internet, you need to first install a virtual switch in Hyper-V. Later when you create a VM, you can connect the VM to the virtual switch, which gives access to the local network and on to the Internet. To create a virtual switch, in the Actions pane, click **Virtual Switch Manager**.

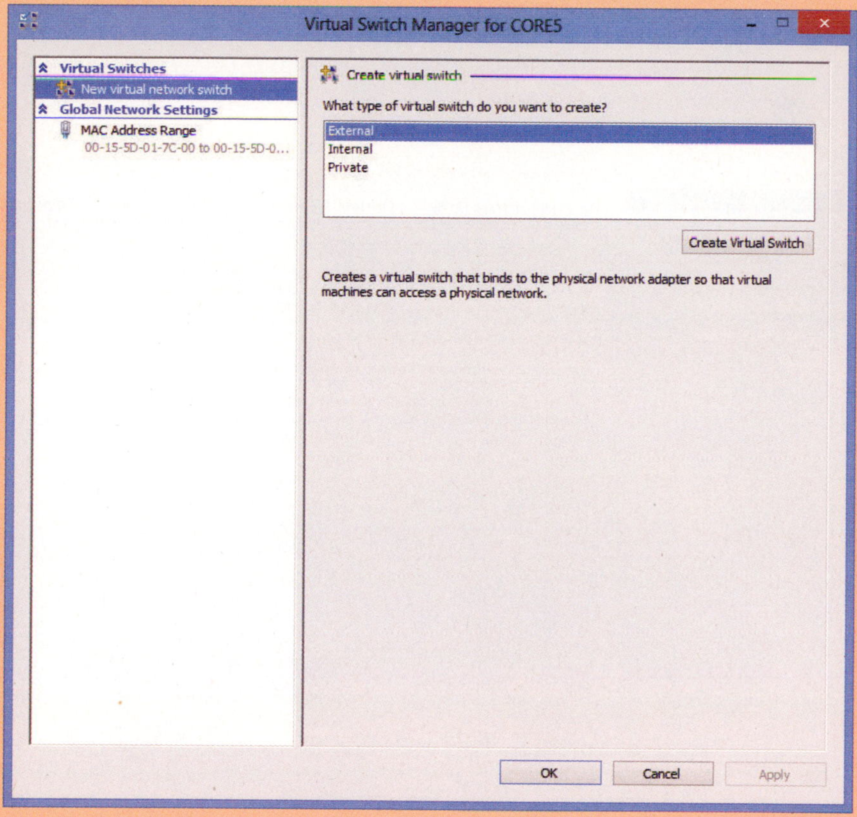

Figure 2-37 Create a new virtual switch
Used with permission from Microsoft Corporation

5. The Virtual Switch Manager dialog box appears (see Figure 2-37). In the left pane, make sure **New virtual network switch** is selected. To bind the virtual switch to the physical network adapter so the VMs can access the physical network, click **External** in the right pane. Click **Create Virtual Switch**.

6. In the Virtual Switch Properties pane that appears, you can name the virtual switch or leave the default name. You can also select the network adapter to use for the switch. For most situations, that would be the wired Ethernet adapter. Make sure **Allow management operating system to share this network adapter** is checked, and then click **Apply**. Click **Yes** and the virtual switch is created. Click **OK** to close the dialog box.

7. You're now ready to create a VM. In the Actions pane, click **New**, and then click **Virtual Machine**. The New Virtual Machine Wizard launches where you can set the name and location of the VM files and configure memory and the virtual hard drive. Click **Next**. (Notice you can click *Finish* to accept default settings for the VM.)

8. In the next dialog box, assign a name to the VM. If you want the VM files stored in a different location than the default, check **Store the virtual machine in a different location**, and browse to that location (see Figure 2-38). When done, click **Next** to move to the next box.

> **Notes** To maintain backups of your VM, be sure to store the VM in a folder that is included in your backup routine.

9. The next box gives you the options of two generations for the VM. Generation 1 uses IDE for boot devices, and supports 32-bit or 64-bit guest operating systems. Generation 2 is new with Windows 8.1, uses SCSI for boot devices, includes the ability to boot the VM from over the network, and requires 64-bit guest operating systems. If you're not sure which to use, select **Generation 1**. Click **Next** to continue.

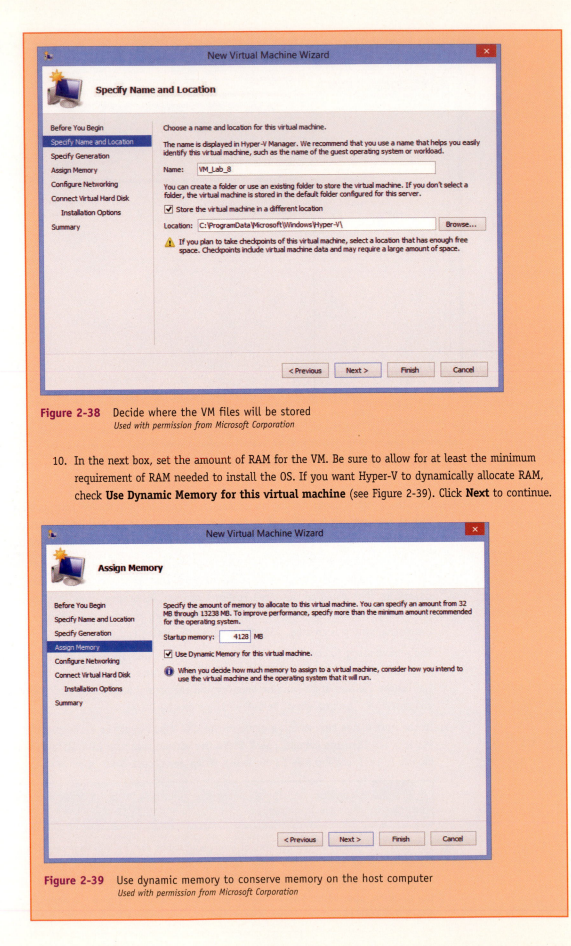

Figure 2-38 Decide where the VM files will be stored
Used with permission from Microsoft Corporation

10. In the next box, set the amount of RAM for the VM. Be sure to allow for at least the minimum requirement of RAM needed to install the OS. If you want Hyper-V to dynamically allocate RAM, check **Use Dynamic Memory for this virtual machine** (see Figure 2-39). Click **Next** to continue.

Figure 2-39 Use dynamic memory to conserve memory on the host computer
Used with permission from Microsoft Corporation

11. In the *Configure Networking* box, select the virtual switch you created earlier, and click **Next**.

12. In the *Connect Virtual Hard Disk* box (see Figure 2-40), you can create a new dynamically expanding virtual hard disk, use an existing virtual disk, or create the VM with no virtual hard disk attached. Make your selections, and click **Next**.

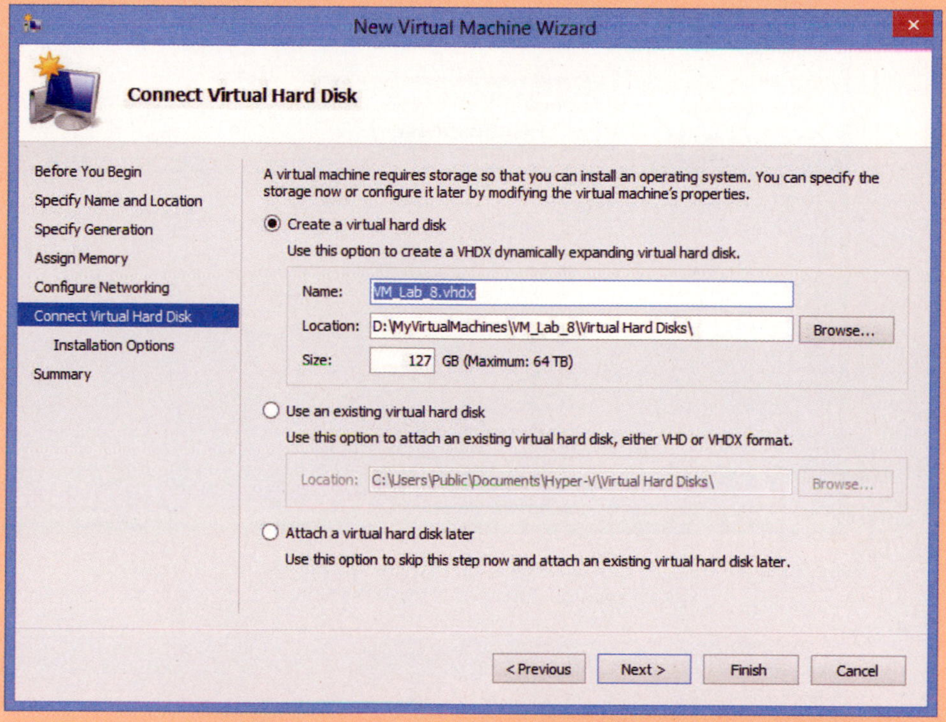

Figure 2-40 Configure the virtual hard disk for the VM
Used with permission from Microsoft Corporation

13. In the *Installation Options* box, decide how you will install an OS in the VM. For example, in Figure 2-41, the OS will be installed from the bootable DVD using an ISO image file as the media. Notice the file has an .iso file extension. Click **Next** to continue. The last box shows a summary of your selections. Click **Finish** to create the VM. The new VM is listed in the Virtual Machines pane in the Hyper-V Manager window.

14. To manage the VM's virtual hardware, select the VM in Hyper-V Manager, and click **Settings** near the bottom of the Actions pane. The Settings box for the VM appears. Select the hardware in the left pane, and apply your settings in the right pane. For example, in Figure 2-42, the DVD Drive is selected. Using the right pane you can mount a physical CD or DVD to the drive or you can mount an ISO file as shown in the figure.

15. If you want to install an OS in the VM by booting the VM to the virtual DVD drive, you need to make sure the VM's BIOS settings have the correct boot priority order. Use the Settings box shown in Figure 2-42 to verify this BIOS setting for the VM. To view and change this setting, click **BIOS** in the left pane.

16. Close the Settings box. To start the VM, select it, and click **Start** in the Actions pane. The VM boots up, and you can then install an OS. A thumbnail of the VM appears in the bottom-middle pane of the Hyper-V Manager window. To see the VM in its own window, double-click the thumbnail. Figure 2-43 shows the VM window at the beginning of the OS installation. Notice in the figure several VMs have been created, and five of them are currently running.

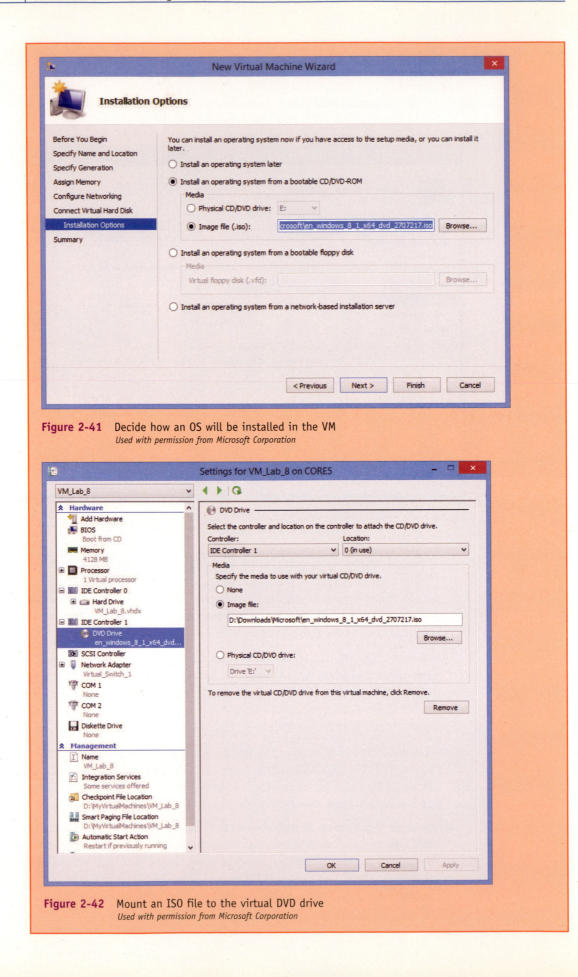

Figure 2-41   Decide how an OS will be installed in the VM
Used with permission from Microsoft Corporation

Figure 2-42   Mount an ISO file to the virtual DVD drive
Used with permission from Microsoft Corporation

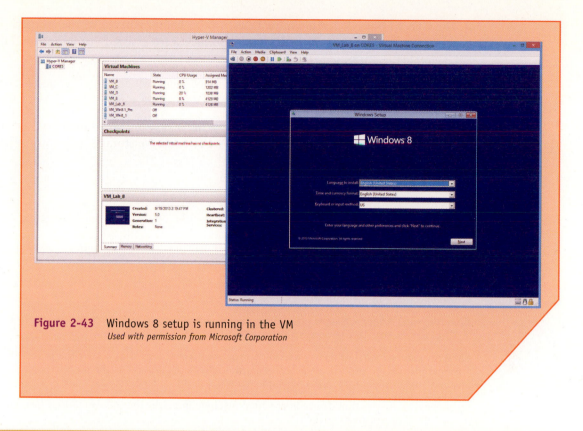

Figure 2-43 Windows 8 setup is running in the VM
Used with permission from Microsoft Corporation

2

>> CHAPTER SUMMARY

Installing Windows 8

- Windows 8 has about the same minimum hardware requirements as Windows 7, except computers older than 10 years will most likely not qualify

- Editions of Windows 8 are Windows RT (uses an ARM processor), Windows 8, Windows 8 Professional, and Windows 8 Enterprise. All editions come in 32 or 64-bit versions.

- You can use an upgrade license of Windows 8 for a Windows 7/Vista/XP computer. For Windows Vista or XP, you must perform a clean install of Windows 8. You must perform a clean install when installing Windows 8.1 on a Windows 7 computer.

- You can install Windows 8 as an upgrade, clean install, or dual boot. An in-place upgrade of Windows 8 must be launched from within Windows 7 using a Windows 8 DVD or files downloaded from the Web.

- After the installation, verify you have network access, activate Windows, install updates for Windows (including Windows 8.1 if it's not already installed), verify automatic update settings are as you want them, install hardware and applications, set up user accounts and transfer or restore from backup user data and preferences, turn Windows features on or off, and, for a mobile computer, verify power management settings.

Installing and Using Virtual Machines with Client Hyper-V

- Client Hyper-V is embedded in 64-bit Windows 8 Professional. It uses a virtual switch, dynamically expanding virtual hard drives, and dynamically allocated memory.

- Beginning with Windows 8.1, Client Hyper-V offers two generations of VMs. Generation 1 VMs support 32-bit and 64-bit installations of an OS, and Generation 2 VMs can only host 64-bit operating systems.

▲ The Client Hyper-V feature must be turned on before you use it, the motherboard and processor must support virtualization, and hardware-assisted virtualization (HAV) must be enabled in BIOS setup

▲ To allow your VMs in Client Hyper-V to have network and Internet access, you must configure a virtual switch and connect each VM to the switch

▲ Use dynamic memory in a VM to conserve the host computer's memory. Use a dynamically expanding virtual hard drive in a VM to conserve storage space on the host computer's hard drive.

>> KEY TERMS

dynamic memory – Memory assigned to a virtual machine that ties up only the portion of allocated memory in the host computer that the VM is actually using.

NX (Never Execute or No Execute) – A processor technology that helps prevent malware from hiding and executing in the data storage area of a program.

PAE (Physical Address Extension) – A processor technology required when a processor is running in 32-bit mode so NX can access all the memory addresses in a system.

SSE2 (Streaming SIMD Extensions 2) – A processor technology that allows the processor to receive a single instruction and then execute it on multiple pieces of data as the data streams through. SIMD stands for "single instruction, multiple data."

virtual switch – A virtual device in a virtual machine manager that allows virtual machines to connect to a physical network.

Windows 8 Enterprise – An edition of Windows 8 that allows for volume licensing in an enterprise and includes Windows to Go.

Windows 8 Professional – An edition of Windows 8 that includes BitLocker, Client Hyper-V, Group Policy, and the ability to join a domain and host Remote Desktop.

>> REVIEWING THE BASICS

1. What three processor technologies are required to install Windows 8?

2. Why does Microsoft require these three processor technologies, even though they are currently available on all processors sold today?

3. What are the three editions of Windows 8?

4. Following the initial release of Windows 8, what is the name of the next release that included major updates for the OS?

5. How can you find out if a system qualifies for a Windows 8 upgrade?

6. At what point does Microsoft verify that a Windows 8 product key is valid for a clean install of the OS rather than an upgrade?

7. When you download the Windows 8 setup files from the Microsoft website, how can you save the files and later use them to create a bootable Windows 8 setup DVD?

8. What are the two basic settings for network security?

9. Which option on the Quick Launch menu can you use to troubleshoot a network connection?

10. Which window do you use to control which apps can make incoming network connections on the network?

11. Which window do you use to find out if the Windows 8 installation has been activated?

12. List the steps to open the Windows Update window.

13. By default, when and how often does the first release of Windows 8 automatically install updates? When does Windows 8.1 automatically install updates?

14. If you already own Windows 8, how much does the Windows 8.1 release cost?

15. Which window can you use to uninstall applications that use the Windows desktop?

16. What are the hardware requirements needed to run Client Hyper-V?

17. How does a VM connect to the physical network when using Client Hyper-V?

18. What is an advantage of using dynamic memory in a VM?

19. Which generation of VM's in Client Hyper-V can only use 64-bit installations for the guest OS?

20. Which type of file can you use to mount a virtual image of a DVD to the virtual optical drive in a virtual machine?

>> THINKING CRITICALLY

1. Suppose you have Windows XP installed on your computer and purchase the upgrade license of Windows 8. Using this license, which ways can you install Windows 8?

   a. You can perform only an upgrade, but not a clean install.

   b. You can perform an upgrade or a clean install.

   c. You can perform only a clean install, but not an upgrade.

   d. In this situation, you cannot install Windows 8 using the upgrade license. You must go back and purchase the full license of Windows 8.

2. Suppose you have 32-bit Windows 7 Home Premium installed on your computer, and you purchase the upgrade license of Windows 8 Professional. You want to install Windows 8 using a 64-bit installation. Which ways can you install Windows 8?

   a. You can perform only an upgrade, but not a clean install.

   b. You can perform an upgrade or a clean install.

   c. You can perform only a clean install, but not an upgrade.

   d. In this situation, you cannot install Windows 8 using the upgrade license. You must go back and purchase the full license of Windows 8.

3. After attempting to start up a virtual machine in the Hyper-V Manager window, you get an error message that says, "Virtual machine could not be started because the hypervisor is not running." Which of the following is most likely to be the problem?

   a. The hypervisor software has not yet been downloaded and installed from the Microsoft website.

   b. The VM does not have enough memory allotted to it.

   c. The hypervisor service has not yet been started using the Services console.

   d. Hardware-assisted virtualization has not yet been enabled in BIOS setup.

4. A laptop reports that it has made a wireless network connection, but it cannot access the network or the Internet. Arrange the following steps in the best order to troubleshoot the problem:

   a. Use Device Manager to uninstall the wireless adapter and install it again.

   b. Disable and enable the wireless network adapter.

   c. Disconnect the connection, and connect again to the wireless network.

   d. Use Device Manager to update the wireless adapter drivers.

>> HANDS-ON PROJECTS

PROJECT 2-1: Install 64-bit Windows 8 Pro

Following directions in the chapter, install 64-bit Windows 8 Professional on your lab computer. If you need help with the installation, see the directions in the chapter or follow the steps in the labs in Lab B near the end of this book. Set up Windows to use a local account to sign in to Windows.

PROJECT 2-2: Perform Routine Maintenance

Do the following to perform routine maintenance chores on Windows 8:

1. Open **Windows Defender**, and make sure real-time protection is turned on. When were malware definitions last updated?

2. Do a disk cleanup on the Windows volume (most likely drive C:).

3. Open **Device Manager**, and use it to update the drivers for installed devices.

4. Use the **Windows Update** window to verify that Windows is set to automatically download and install important updates.

5. Open the **Network and Sharing Center**. Is the network configured as a private network or public network?

PROJECT 2-3: Install Windows 8 in a VM

This project assumes you already have 64-bit Windows 8 Pro installed on a computer. Do the following:

1. Enable Client Hyper-V, and set up a VM in it.

2. Install Windows 8 in the VM.

3. Verify you can use Internet Explorer in the VM to surf the Web.

PROJECT 2-4: Use a Virtual Machine

To practice networking skills with Windows 8 in a VM, work with a partner who is working on a different computer than yours. Do the following:

1. Using the VM you created in Project 2-3, join the VM on your computer with the VM on your partner's computer into a homegroup. What is the password to the homegroup?

2. Put a file in the Documents library of your VM. Any file will do. Rename the file so your name is part of the file name. Share the Documents library with the homegroup.

3. Copy the file in the Documents library on your partner's VM to your Documents library in your VM.

> **Notes** If you are working alone with only one computer, you can use two virtual machines installed on the same computer to do this project.

PROJECT 2-5:   Research Windows 8

When Microsoft releases a new OS, those in the technical community begin to tinker with it and post blogs and forums about the OS. Search the Web to find or answer the following:

1. Find a funny joke or cartoon about Windows 8. Share it with your class. Based on the types of jokes and cartoons you find, what is the technical community's perception of Windows 8?

2. Find freeware that makes the Start button in Windows 8 work as it did in Windows 7 so it lists installed programs for you to launch. What is the name of the freeware and the URL where you can get it?

3. What are 10 shortcuts, such as Win+X or Alt+F, that you might find useful when working with Windows 8? List the shortcut and what it does.

4. List the steps to add contacts to the People app. What is the advantage of putting all your contacts in the People app?

5. List the steps to connect your Facebook account to your People app.

>> REAL PROBLEMS, REAL SOLUTIONS

REAL PROBLEM 2-1:   Document How to Use Windows 8

In Chapter 1, you created a screen recording of how to use Windows 8. Using a microphone, an optional web cam, and the Screencast-O-Matic software you installed in Real Problem 1-1 in Chapter 1, make a second recording that covers one of the following topics:

- How to decide if your computer qualifies for Windows 8

- How to install Windows 8 as a dual boot (this screen recording works well when you're using a virtual machine for the installation)

- How to check for and install Windows updates

- Any other topic approved by your instructor

The recording should be no longer than three minutes. Save the file in the MP4 format.

REAL PROBLEM 2-2:   Install a Shortcut Tile on the Start Screen

The Windows 8 shutdown and startup processes are fast because Windows doesn't complete a full shutdown but rather goes into a type of hibernation. If you're having problems with Windows 8, you might want to perform a full-function shutdown. To do so, you can use the **shutdown -s -t 0** command. To do so, open the Quick Launch menu, click **Run**, enter the command in the Run dialog box, and click **OK**. To make the command easily accessible, you can create a shortcut on the desktop and a tile on the Start screen to perform the shutdown. Do the following:

1. To verify the command parameters work, practice the shutdown command using the Run dialog box.

2. Create a shortcut on the desktop that contains the **shutdown -s -t 0** command. (Hint: Right-click the desktop, and select an option from the shortcut menu.)

3. Name the shortcut **Full Shutdown**.

4. Change the icon for the shortcut to the power icon. (Hint: Right-click the shortcut, and select an option from the shortcut menu.)

5. Pin the shortcut to the Start screen. Figure 2-44 shows the Full Shutdown tile with the power icon on the Start screen. (Hint: Right-click the shortcut, and select an option from the shortcut menu.)

6. Take a screenshot of the tile on the Start screen to send to your instructor. In a computer lab, remove the shortcut from the desktop and the tile from the Start screen.

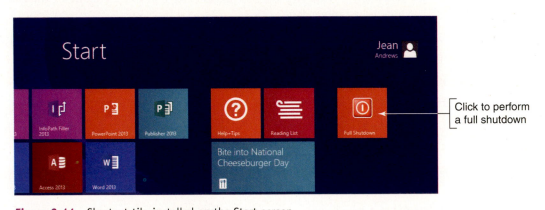

Figure 2-44 Shortcut tile installed on the Start screen
Used with permission from Microsoft Corporation

CHAPTER 3

Maintaining and Troubleshooting Windows 8

When a new operating system first comes on the market, computer support technicians must quickly learn how to maintain, secure, and troubleshoot it. This chapter helps you do just that. In general, Windows provides maintenance, security, and troubleshooting tools in two locations: in the Windows 8 interface and on the desktop. As you'll see in the chapter, when these tools are accessed from the Windows 8 interface, not all features of a tool are available to the user. The Windows 8 interface tools are designed so that end users can make simple changes to the system and can easily follow directions from a support technician on the phone. On the other hand, when a tool is accessed from the desktop, a support technician can find every feature a tool has to offer, and more expertise is needed to use these features. You need to be familiar with both methods of accessing tools because most support technicians find they must teach end users how to fix simple problems, and, when providing phone support, you want your instructions to be as easy as possible for your client or customer to follow.

In this chapter, you'll first learn how to maintain a Windows 8 computer by learning about the new Task Manager, the backup and restore tools new to Windows 8, and new methods to protect against malware. Then you'll learn to use the several new tools and techniques included in Windows 8 that can help you solve a Windows problem and troubleshoot a corrupted Windows installation.

> **Notes** Labs to accompany this chapter can be found in Lab C near the back of this book.

> **Notes** This chapter is written to follow Chapter 18 in *A+ Guide to Managing and Maintaining Your PC, 8th Edition*, or Chapter 9 in *A+ Guide to Software, 6th Edition*.

MAINTAINING WINDOWS 8

When learning to maintain a new operating system, you can build on your knowledge and experience gained from supporting previous OSs. Windows 8 has an architecture similar to that of Windows 7, and the folder structures are also the same. The important folders you need to know about are listed below. These folders are the same as in Windows 7, and it's assumed Windows is installed on drive C.

▲ User profiles are kept in the C:\Users folder
▲ For a 32-bit Windows installation, program files for applications are stored in the C:\Program Files folder
▲ For a 64-bit Windows installation, program files for applications are stored here:

  • Program files for 64-bit applications are stored in the C:\Program Files folder

  • Program files for 32-bit applications are stored in the C:\Program Files (x86) folder

▲ Windows is stored in C:\Windows, and the folder structure within this folder is the same as in Windows 7

> **Notes** The instructions in this chapter assume that you are using a mouse and keyboard. If you're using a touch screen, simply tap instead of click; press and hold instead of right-click; double-tap instead of double-click; and swipe to scroll the screen to the right or left.

Now let's look at the new Task Manager, the Windows 8 backup, restore, and system recovery tools, as well as tools used to protect against malware.

THE NEW TASK MANAGER

Task Manager has several changes from Windows 7. As with Windows 7, to open Task Manager, you can press **Ctrl+Alt+Delete** or right-click the taskbar on the desktop and then click **Task Manager**. In Windows 8, you can also press **Win+X**, and click **Task Manager** in the Quick Launch menu. The Task Manager window is shown in Figure 3-1. If you see very limited information in the window, click **More details** to see the details shown in the figure.

> **Notes** The figures and steps in this book use Windows 8.1 Professional. If you are using a different edition of Windows 8, your screens and steps may differ slightly from those presented here.

Let's take a look at the Task Manager tabs.

PROCESSES TAB AND DETAILS TAB

The Processes tab shows running processes organized by Apps, Background processes, and Windows processes. Right-click a process, and click **Go to details** (see Figure 3-1) to jump to the Details tab where you see the name of the program file and other details about the running program.

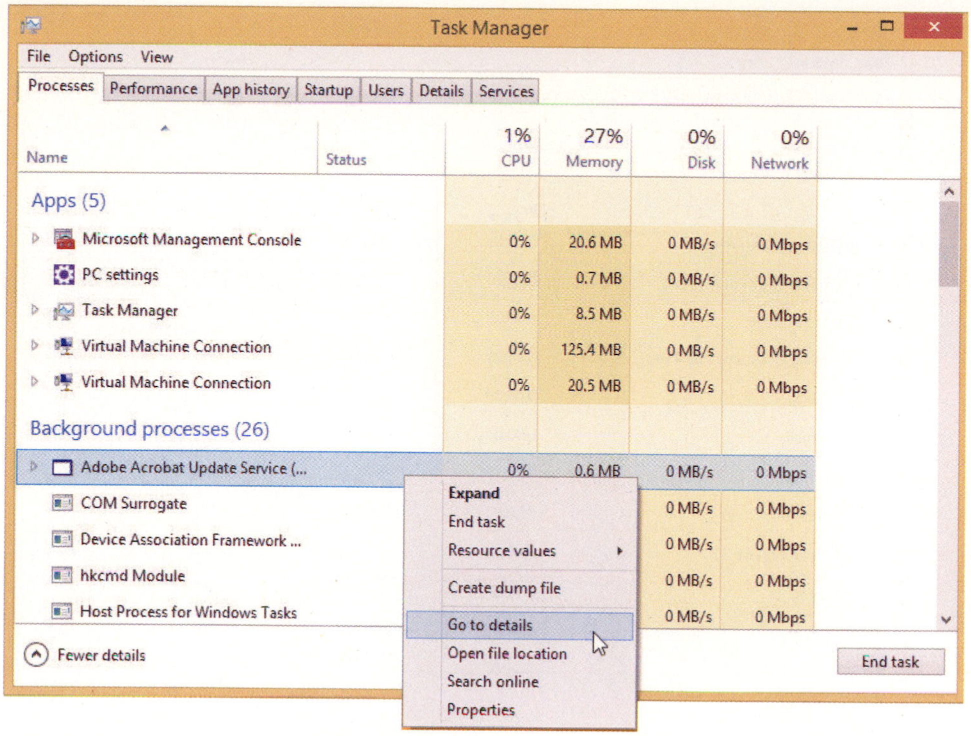

Figure 3-1   The Windows 8 Task Manager window
Used with permission from Microsoft Corporation

APP HISTORY TAB

The App history tab (see Figure 3-2) shows the resources that a program is using. For example, it is useful when deciding if a live tile for an app on the Start screen is using up too many system resources when providing live information on the tile. If you want to disable a live tile from updating itself, go to the **Start** screen, right-click the tile, and click **Turn live tile off** in the status bar.

PERFORMANCE TAB AND USERS TAB

The Performance tab of Task Manager (see Figure 3-3) combines information previously given on the Performance and Networking tabs of the Windows 7 Task Manager. In addition, on this tab you can monitor the performance of all installed hard drives. Click **Open Resource Monitor** on this tab to open the Resource Monitor, which works the same as in Windows 7. If you suspect CPU, memory, disk, or network resources are being used excessively by a process, you can use Resource Monitor to identify the process. Check for such a process if you suspect malware might be at work in a denial-of-service (DoS) attack.

The Users tab (see Figure 3-4) gives performance information that can help you identify processes started by a signed-in user that might be affecting overall system performance. Notice that the statuses of some programs on this tab are listed as Suspended. In Windows 8, if certain apps remain idle for a short time, they're suspended so they don't require the attention of the CPU. When the app is used again, it automatically comes out of suspension, and the CPU once again begins servicing it.

> **Notes** On the Users tab of Task Manager, you might need to click the white arrow beside a user account name to expand the view so you can see processes running under the user account.

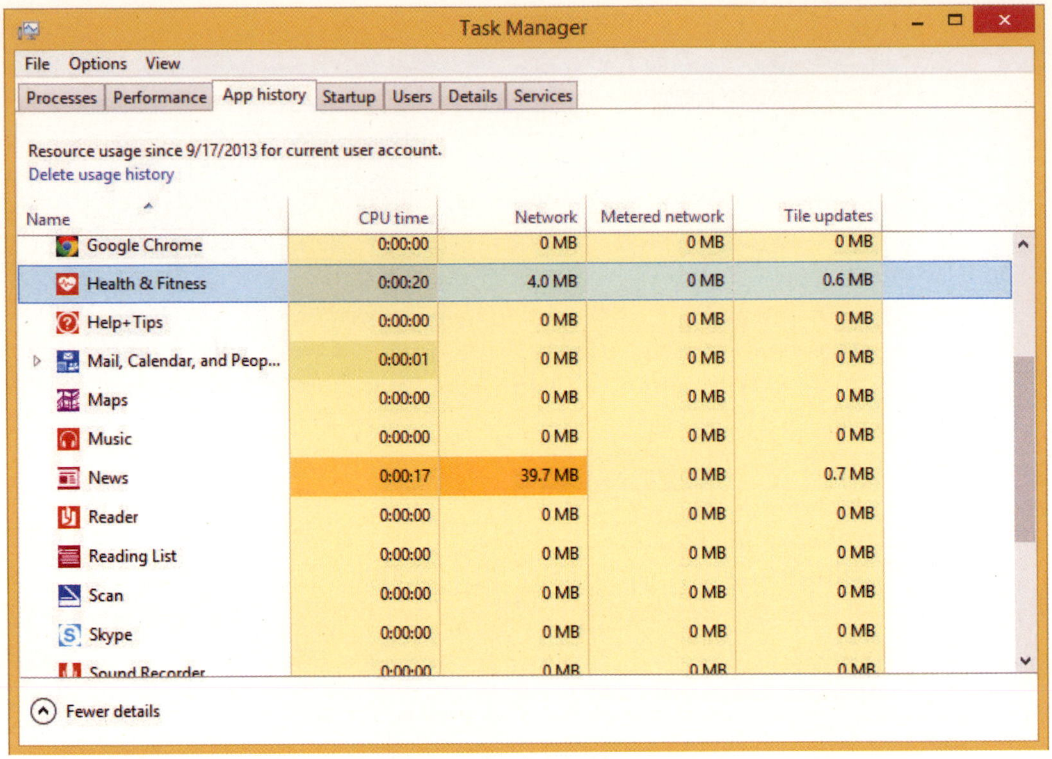

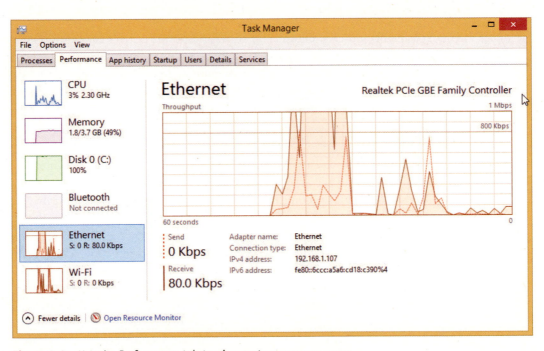

Figure 3-2   The App history tab can help you decide if a background program is hogging system resources
Used with permission from Microsoft Corporation

Figure 3-3   Use the Performance tab to view system resource usage
Used with permission from Microsoft Corporation

STARTUP TAB

The Startup tab of Task Manager in Windows 8 is used to manage startup items (see the foreground window in Figure 3-5). To disable a program from launching at startup, select it, and click **Disable** at the bottom of the window or in the shortcut menu. To see the

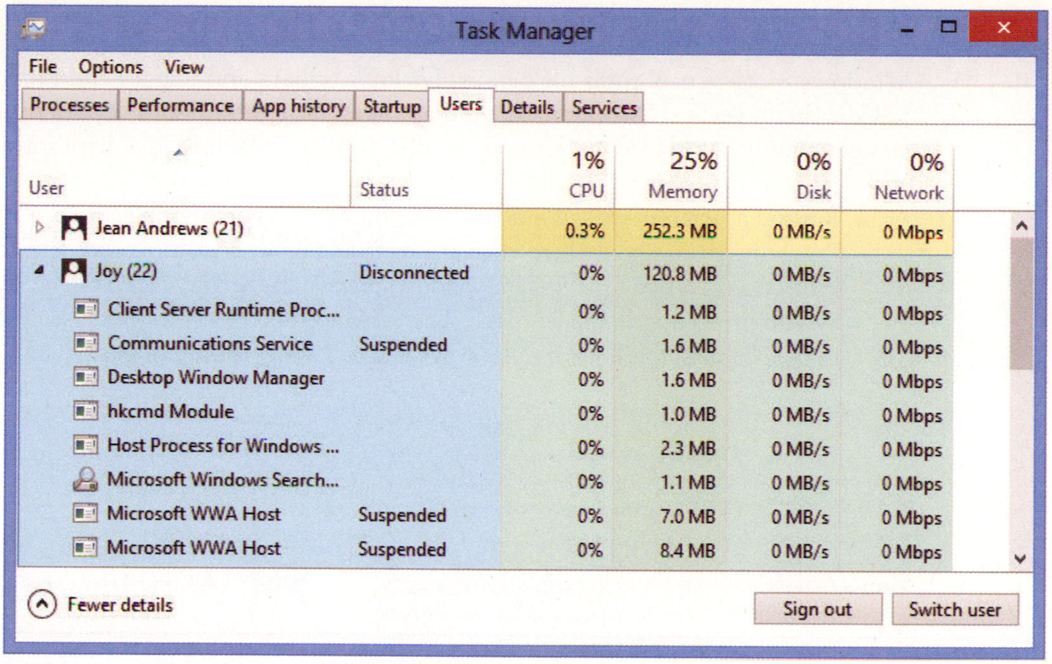

Figure 3-4 The Users tab shows system resources used by each signed-in user
Used with permission from Microsoft Corporation

3

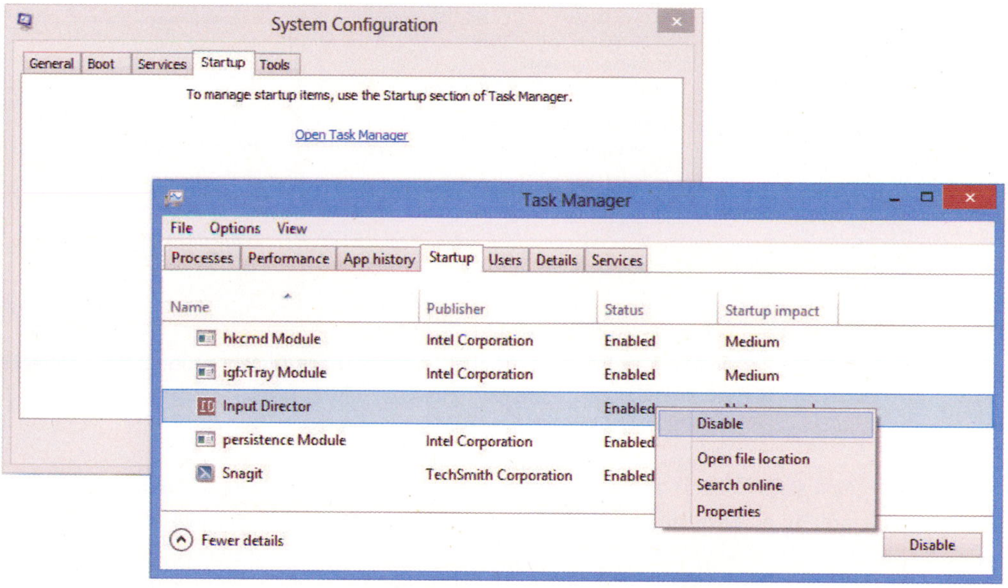

Figure 3-5 Startup processes are managed on the Startup tab of Task Manager
Used with permission from Microsoft Corporation

program file location, right-click it, and click **Open file location,** as shown in the figure. Also notice in the figure the Startup tab in the Windows 8 System Configuration window shown in the background. The message and link on this tab remind us that System Configuration in Windows 8 is no longer used to manage startup programs.

Notes To open the System Configuration window, press **Win+X**, click **Run**, type **msconfig** in the Run dialog box, and press **Enter**. Alternately, you can go to the Start screen, type **System Configuration**, and select **System Configuration** from the results.

WINDOWS 8 BACKUP AND RECOVERY METHODS

Windows 8 offers new tools for making backups of data and images and for recovering a failed system, yet it still supports the old methods. You'll find many options and tools, which can get confusing. Before we get into the details of how each works, here's a summary list:

▲ *Restore points:* As with Windows 7, use the System window to get to the System Properties dialog box where you can create and apply a restore point and configure System Protection. To open the System window, press **Win+X**, and click **System**. Then click **System protection** in the left pane. The System Properties box opens (see Figure 3-6). Later in the chapter, you'll learn other ways you can apply restore points.

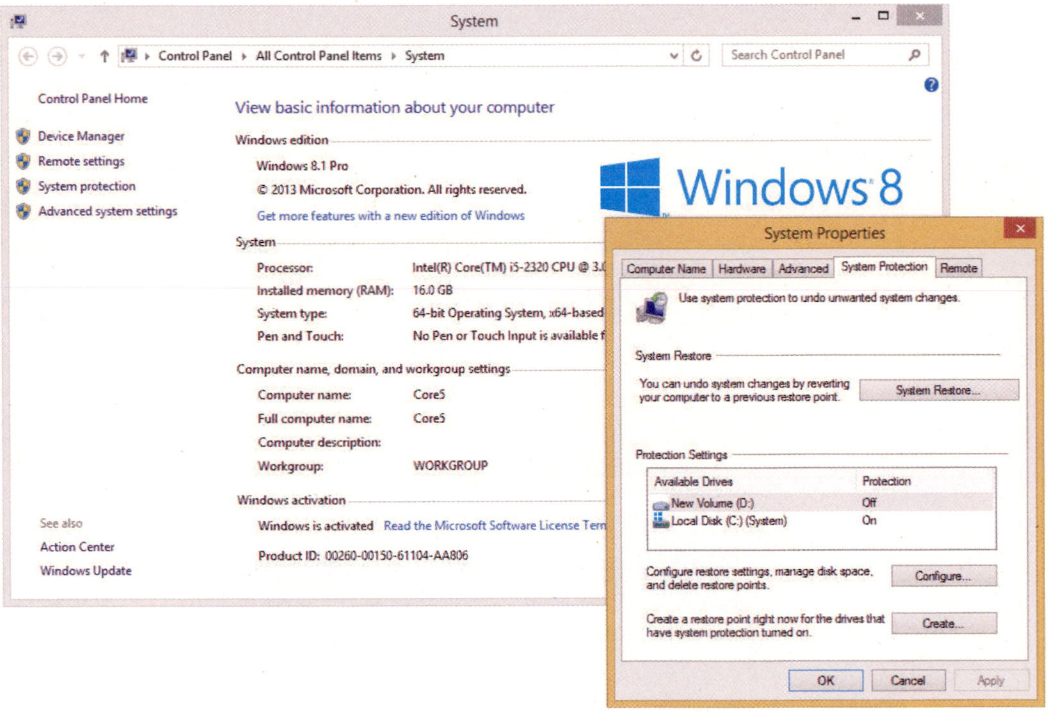

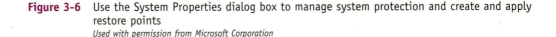

Figure 3-6 Use the System Properties dialog box to manage system protection and create and apply restore points
Used with permission from Microsoft Corporation

? To Learn More To learn more about creating and using restore points, start at page 457 in Chapter 10 of *A+ Guide to Managing and Maintaining Your PC, 8th edition*, or page 113 in Chapter 3 of *A+ Guide to Software, 6th edition*.

▲ *File History:* **File History** is new to Windows 8 and is used to back up and restore personal data folders and files to a specified drive and to create system images. It's intended to replace the Windows 7 Backup and Restore Center.

▲ *Reset Windows:* The Settings charm and boot media offer the option to reset Windows. When you **reset Windows**, the Windows volume is formatted and Windows is reinstalled. If a recovery partition is provided by the computer manufacturer, the system is reset to its factory state. If there's no recovery partition, the process requests the Windows setup DVD, which it uses to reinstall Windows. All user data and settings and installed apps are lost. Consider a reset your last-ditch effort to fix a corrupted Windows installation.

▲ *Refresh Windows:* The Settings charm and boot media also offer the option to refresh Windows. When you **refresh Windows**, Windows first backs up user settings, personal data files, and apps that use the Windows 8 interface. Then it formats the Windows volume, reinstalls Windows, and restores user settings, data files, and apps from backup. Depending on how the refresh is done, desktop applications might be lost. When troubleshooting a system, always try a refresh before you reset the system.

▲ *Custom refresh images:* You can create one or more custom refresh images to be used when you refresh Windows. A **custom refresh image** is similar to a system image used in Windows 7 and is intended to replace system images as the method for backing up the Windows volume. It includes everything installed or written on the Windows volume, including user data and settings, Windows 8 apps, and desktop applications.

▲ *Recovery drive:* Using Windows 7, you can create a system repair disc that can be used to boot up and repair the system. In Windows 8, you can create a bootable USB flash drive for the same purpose, called a **recovery drive**. If the computer manufacturer provided a recovery partition on the hard drive, you can copy this recovery partition to the USB flash drive. The flash drive can then be used to reset the hard drive back to its factory state even when the recovery partition has been corrupted or deleted or the entire hard drive has been replaced. When you first become responsible for a laptop or tablet device, it's a good idea to create a recovery drive before problems occur.

Now let's see how to use the new stuff. We'll see how File History works, how to reset and refresh a computer, and how to create and use a custom refresh image and a recovery drive.

USE FILE HISTORY

The File History utility is intended to replace the Windows 7 Backup and Restore Center for backing up personal data files and folders and creating system images. It's easy to use and is designed with the nontechnical end user in mind.

By default, File History backs up libraries, user desktops, contacts, SkyDrives (for Microsoft accounts), and Internet Explorer favorites. Backups can be kept on an external hard drive, a USB flash drive, or a drive on the network.

The File History utility is available as a window on the Windows desktop or an app in the Windows 8 interface. To view and change advanced settings for File History and to create system images, you need to use the window on the desktop. Follow these steps:

1. First connect your backup device. Open **Control Panel** in icon view (see Figure 3-7), and then click **File History**.

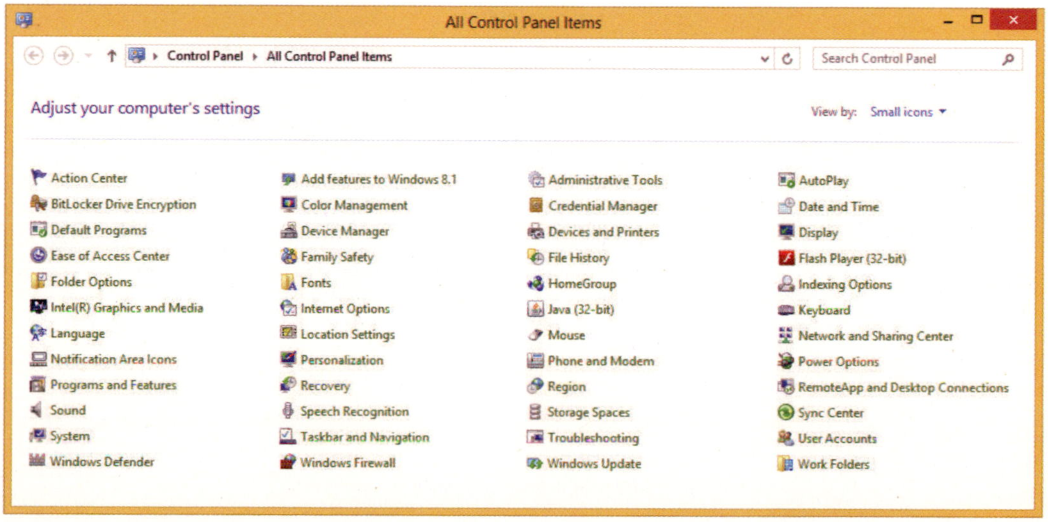

Figure 3-7 Windows 8 Control Panel in Small icons view
Used with permission from Microsoft Corporation

2. Figure 3-8 shows a File History window that recognizes a drive to hold the backups. The drive in the figure is an external hard drive with plenty of free space. To turn on File History, click **Turn on**. By default, File History backs up every hour and keeps as many generations of backups as it has free space on the storage device.

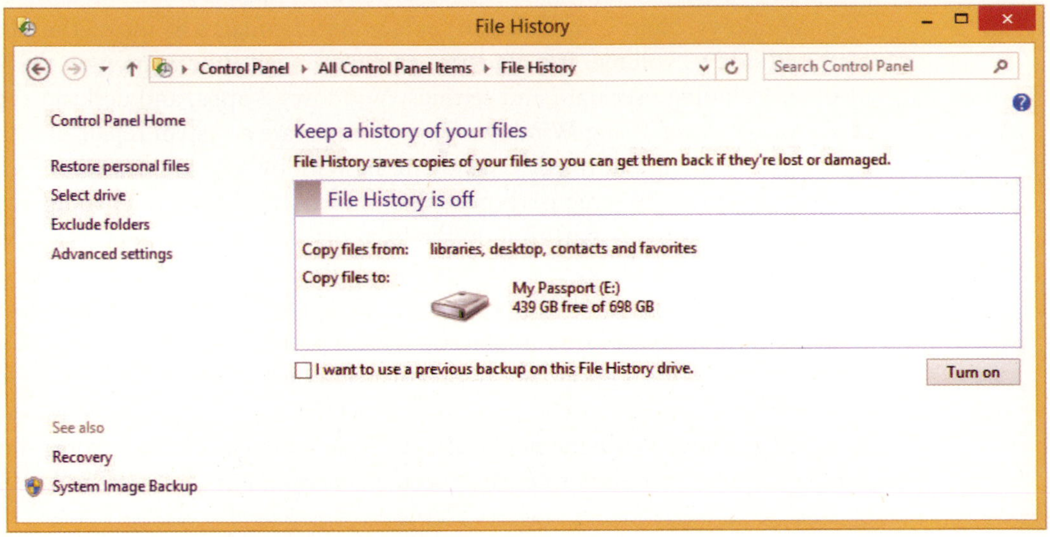

Figure 3-8 Turn on and off File History and control its settings
Used with permission from Microsoft Corporation

3. To manage these backups, click **Advanced settings**. On the Advanced Settings window (see Figure 3-9), you can set how often backups are made (every 10 minutes up to daily) and how long old backups should be kept (forever, until space is needed, 1 month, 1 year, and so forth). You can also view a history of events and clean up old backups to free up space.

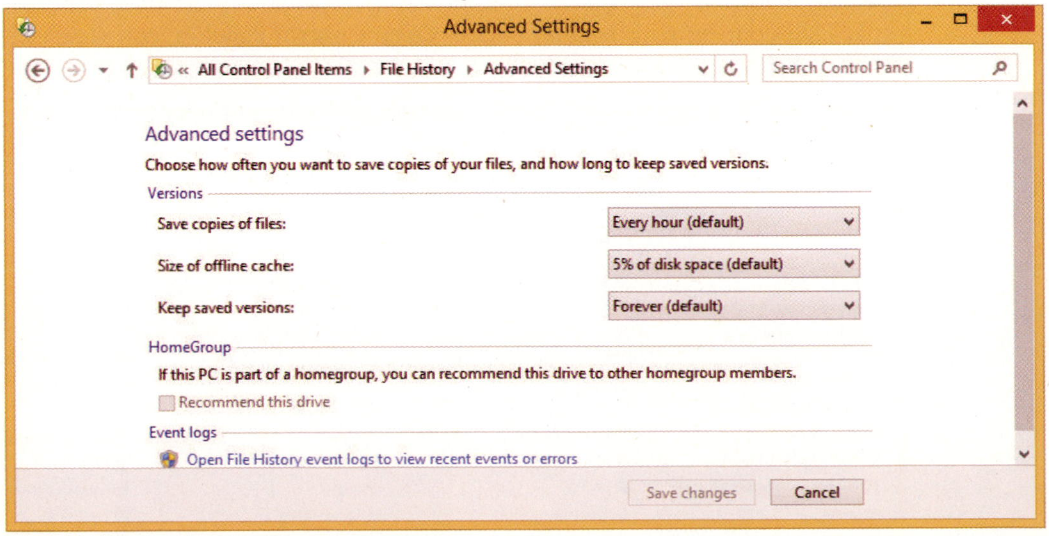

Figure 3-9 File History advanced settings
Used with permission from Microsoft Corporation

To recover items from File History backups, in the File History window, click **Restore personal files**. In the window that appears (see Figure 3-10), drill down into the backups to find the file or folder you need. Select an item, and then click the green button at the bottom of the window to restore it. Before you restore a file or folder, copy the original item to a new location in case you later want to backtrack.

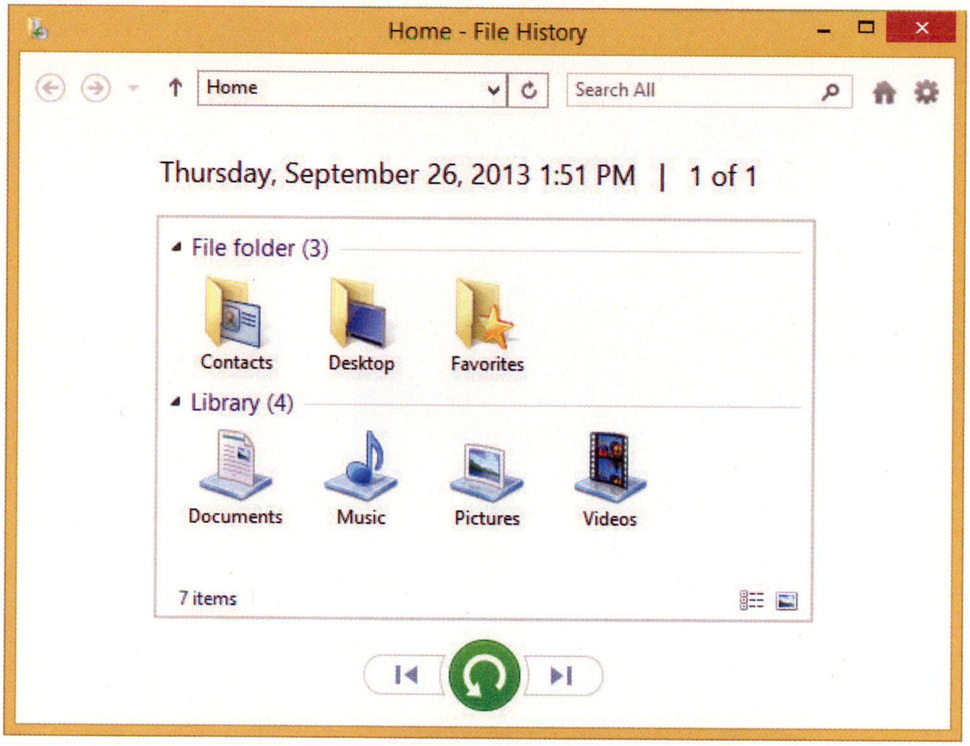

Figure 3-10 Drill down into backups to find what you want to restore
Used with permission from Microsoft Corporation

Recall that a system image is a backup of the entire Windows volume stored in a group of files that can be used to reimage the Windows volume. To create a system image, click **System Image Backup** in the File History window (refer to Figure 3-8). Although Windows 8 supports using system images to recover from a corrupted Windows volume, the newer method is to use a custom refresh image to refresh the computer. You learn how to create and apply a custom refresh image and how to apply a system image later in the chapter.

> **Notes** To open File History in the Windows 8 interface, open the **Settings** charm, and click **Change PC settings**. In the PC settings pane, click **Update and recovery**, and then click **File History**.

RESET A COMPUTER

You might want to reset a computer when you're about to give it away or recycle it or totally want to start over. Computer manufacturers usually provide a recovery partition to reset a laptop, all-in-one, mobile computer, or other brand-name computer to its factory default state. You can use the recovery methods provided by the manufacturer (for example, press F12 or F10 at startup) or you can use Windows 8 to reset the system.

APPLYING CONCEPTS

RESETTING A COMPUTER

Here are the Windows 8 steps to reset a computer:

1. If a recovery partition is present, it will be used for the reset. If there's no recovery partition, insert the Windows setup DVD in the optical drive, which the reset process uses to perform a clean install of Windows.

2. Go to the charms bar, and click **Settings**. In the Settings pane, click **Change PC settings**. In the left pane of the PC settings window (see Figure 3-11), click **Update and recovery**.

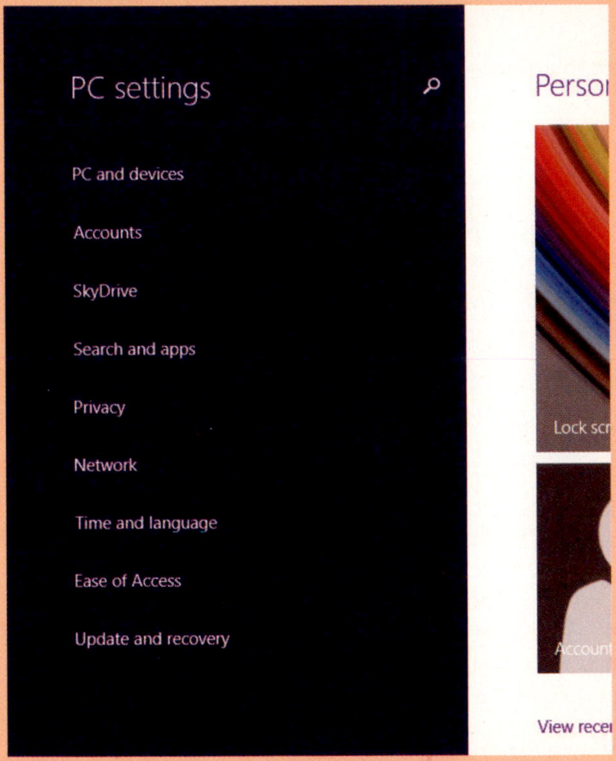

Figure 3-11   Use the Update and recovery link in the PC settings pane
Used with permission from Microsoft Corporation

3. Click **Recovery** (see Figure 3-12). Click **Get started** under *Remove everything and reinstall Windows*. A warning message appears. Click **Next**.

> 📝 **Notes**   You must be signed in as an administrator before you can see all the options on the right side of the Recovery pane.

4. If the system contains more than one volume or hard drive, Windows asks if you want to format all drives or just the Windows volume. Click a box to make your selection.

5. On the next screen (see Figure 3-13), you're asked to decide between a quick format or a thorough format. A thorough format makes it less likely someone can recover data on the drive. Make your selection by clicking a box.

6. On the next screen another warning appears. Click **Reset** to start the process. The system restarts and resetting begins. After another restart, you can step through the process of preparing Windows for first use.

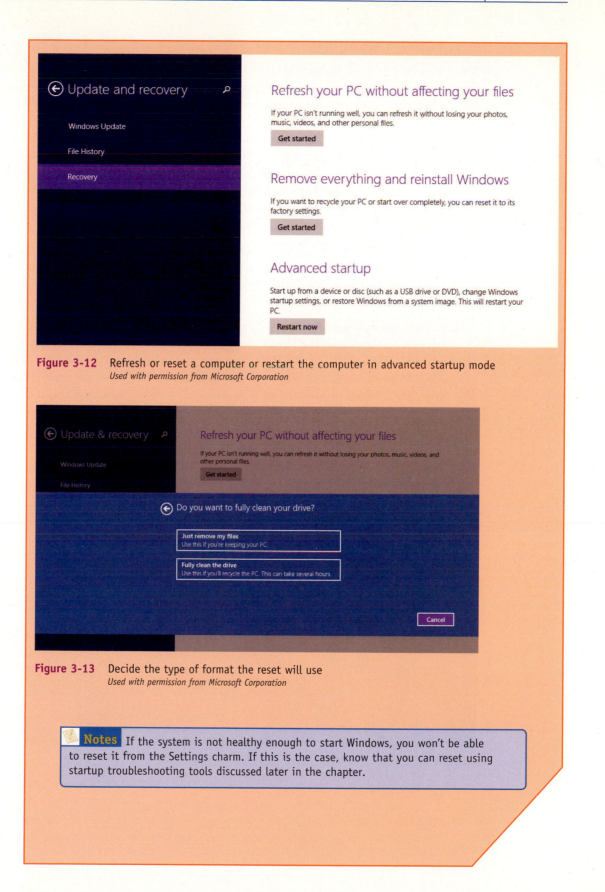

Figure 3-12 Refresh or reset a computer or restart the computer in advanced startup mode
Used with permission from Microsoft Corporation

3

Figure 3-13 Decide the type of format the reset will use
Used with permission from Microsoft Corporation

📝 **Notes** If the system is not healthy enough to start Windows, you won't be able to reset it from the Settings charm. If this is the case, know that you can reset using startup troubleshooting tools discussed later in the chapter.

REFRESH A COMPUTER

When you refresh a computer, the apps that use the Windows 8 interface and user settings and data are kept. Unless you're working with a custom refresh image, Windows settings and desktop applications are lost during a refresh. Here's how to perform a refresh:

1. Because the system will restart a couple times during the refresh, remove any discs in the optical drive and unplug any bootable external hard drive or USB flash drives. For a laptop, plug in the AC adapter so you don't lose battery power during the refresh. If the computer doesn't have a recovery partition and you haven't made a custom refresh image, insert the Windows setup DVD in the optical drive, which the refresh will use to perform a partial in-place upgrade of Windows 8.

2. Go to the **charms** bar, and click **Settings**. Click **Change PC settings**. In the left pane of the PC settings window, click **Update and recovery**, and then click **Recovery**. Click **Get started** under *Refresh your PC without affecting your files* (refer back to Figure 3-12).

3. A warning message appears (see Figure 3-14). Click **Next**. Windows verifies there's enough free space on the hard drive to perform the refresh. A lot of space (as much as half the space on the Windows volume) is needed because Windows will store the old Windows installation in a Windows.old folder and will also need space to back up apps and data. If there's not enough space, an error occurs, and you'll need to delete files or folders or move them to a different location to free up enough space and start the refresh again.

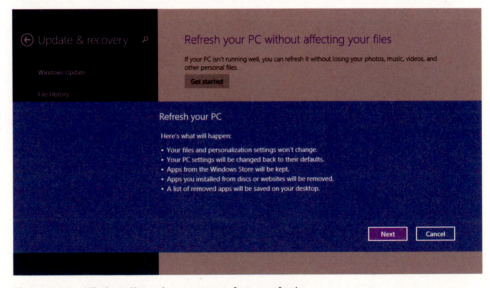

Figure 3-14   Windows lists what to expect from a refresh
Used with permission from Microsoft Corporation

4. Another warning message appears. Click **Refresh** to continue. Next, user settings and data and Windows 8 apps are backed up, and Windows searches for media or an image to use to reinstall Windows. It uses this order for the search:

    a. *It checks for a custom refresh image:* If a custom refresh image (similar to a system image) was previously made and registered with the system, this image is used to refresh the system. (If desktop applications were included in the image, they are included in the refresh. Any desktop applications that were installed after the refresh image was created are lost and must be manually reinstalled.) How to create a custom refresh image is coming up.

b. *If no custom refresh image is found registered in the system, it checks for a recovery partition:* If it finds a recovery partition provided by the computer manufacturer, the image on the partition is used to refresh the computer to its factory state.

c. *If no image or recovery partition is found, it requests the Windows setup DVD:* If Windows can find neither a refresh image nor a recovery partition, it requests the Windows setup DVD and uses it to refresh the computer.

5. The system restarts and the refresh begins. Progress is reported on screen as a percentage of completion. The Windows volume is formatted, and Windows is reinstalled from an image or from the Windows setup files. User settings, data, and Windows 8 apps are then restored from backup, and the system restarts.

6. The names of desktop applications lost during the refresh are stored in a file on the Windows desktop named Removed Apps.html (see Figure 3-15). Open the file to see the list of applications. You'll need to reinstall these applications.

Figure 3-15   View a list of desktop applications lost during the refresh
Used with permission from Microsoft Corporation

7. The refresh created a Windows.old folder containing the old Windows installation. After you're sure you don't need anything in it, you can delete the folder to free up the disk space.

> **Notes** If the system isn't healthy enough to start Windows, you can't do a refresh using the Settings charm. In this case, you can use startup troubleshooting tools to start the system and refresh it. You learn to use these tools later in the chapter.

CREATE A CUSTOM REFRESH IMAGE

Recall that a custom refresh image can be used when refreshing Windows. The image includes everything on the Windows volume including the Windows installation, Windows 8 apps, desktop applications, and user settings and data. The best time to create the image is right after you've installed Windows, hardware, applications, and user accounts and customized Windows settings. The image is stored in a single file named CustomRefresh.wim in the folder you specify. The WIM file uses the Windows Imaging File (WIM) format, which is a compressed file that contains many related files.

Here are the steps to create the custom refresh image:

1. Open an elevated command prompt window. One way to do that is to go to the Apps screen, and right-click **Command Prompt**. In the status bar, click **Run as administrator**. Respond to the UAC box. The Administrator: Command Prompt window opens.

2. Enter this command, substituting any drive and folder for that shown in the command line (see Figure 3-16):

   recimg /createimage D:\MyImage

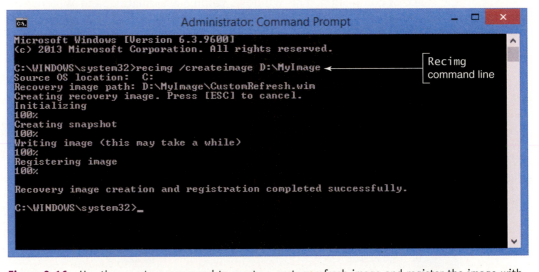

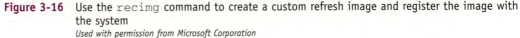

Figure 3-16 Use the `recimg` command to create a custom refresh image and register the image with the system
Used with permission from Microsoft Corporation

Creating the image takes some time. Once completed, the image and its location are registered as the active recovery image. The image is stored in a large file, and you can view it using File Explorer (see Figure 3-17). As you saw earlier, Windows will use the active recovery image during a refresh even if a recovery partition is present.

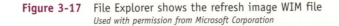

Figure 3-17 File Explorer shows the refresh image WIM file
Used with permission from Microsoft Corporation

The `recimg` command can also be used to manage refresh images. The parameters for the command are listed in Table 3-1.

Command	Description
`recimg /createimage <path>`	Creates the refresh image and registers its location as the active refresh image
`recimg /showcurrent`	Displays the location of the active refresh image
`bcdedit /set {default}` `  bootmenupolicy legacy`	Deregisters the active recovery image; if a recovery partition is present, the partition will then be used for a refresh
`recimg /setcurrent <path>`	Registers a refresh image in the path given; the image at this location is now the active refresh image

Table 3-1 The `recimg` command and parameters

Suppose you've created multiple refresh images and you want to select a particular image for a refresh. Figure 3-18 shows the commands you can use to change the active refresh image from the one stored in the D:\MyImage folder to one stored in the D:\MyImage2 folder.

3

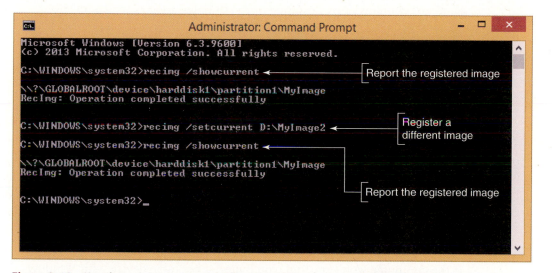

Figure 3-18 Use the `recimg` command with parameters to manage refresh images
Used with permission from Microsoft Corporation

Notes Because a refresh image must be named CustomRefresh.wim, you must store each image in a separate folder.

You might be wondering how a custom refresh image in Windows 8 differs from a system image used in Windows 7 and earlier operating systems. They're similar in that they both contain an image of the Windows volume and can be used only on the computer that created them. Table 3-2 lists the main differences between the two types of images.

	System Image	Custom Refresh Image
How created	Using the File History window	Using the `recimg` command
How stored	Stored as a group of subfolders and files and can receive incremental updates	Stored in a single file named CustomRefresh.wim
How used	To reimage the system to its state when the system image was created	To refresh the system to its state when the refresh image was created and then current user settings, data, and Windows 8 apps are restored

Table 3-2　Differences between a system image and refresh image

? **To Learn More**　To learn more about creating and updating a system image in Windows 7, start at page 450 of Chapter 10 of *A+ Guide to Managing and Maintaining Your PC, 8th Edition*, and page 106 of Chapter 3 of *A+ Guide to Software, 6th Edition*.

? **To Learn More**　To learn more about applying a system image in Windows 7, start at page 678 in Chapter 14 of *A+ Guide to Managing and Maintaining Your PC, 8th Edition*, and page 276 of Chapter 6 of *A+ Guide to Software, 6th Edition*.

The major disadvantage of a refresh image is that it cannot receive incremental updates. Here are two advantages of using a refresh image over a system image:

- When you use a refresh image to refresh a computer, after the refresh image is applied, user data and settings and Windows 8 apps in the current system are automatically carried forward to the refreshed computer
- A refresh is easy to do, and a technician can step an end user through the process over the phone in a troubleshooting situation. If the hard drive has the available space, the image can be stored on the Windows volume so the user doesn't have to deal with recovery media. Basically, it's a powerful, yet simple-to-use, recovery tool.

As a rule of thumb, after you've installed Windows, hardware, and applications and set up user accounts, create a custom refresh image so you can easily refresh the computer to its state after everything is installed, without losing current user data and settings and Windows 8 apps.

CREATE A RECOVERY DRIVE

If the computer won't start up, you'll need a bootable device with Windows repair tools on it to start the system and fix problems. Here are options for that device:

- If the computer has an optical drive, you can boot from the Windows setup DVD and use Windows RE to fix problems

Notes　Recall that the Windows Recovery Environment (Windows RE) is a lean operating system that can be loaded from the Windows setup DVD and is used to troubleshoot Windows when it cannot start from the hard drive.

- You can use a tool new to Windows 8 called a recovery drive. A recovery drive is a bootable USB flash drive that replaces the Windows 7 system repair disc. Many mobile computers don't have an optical drive, which can make a recovery drive an essential troubleshooting tool.

 **Notes** A recovery drive is bit-specific: Use a 32-bit recovery drive to repair a 32-bit Windows installation and a 64-bit recovery drive to repair a 64-bit installation.

If a computer has a recovery partition, you have the option to copy this partition to the recovery drive. If the drive is to hold the recovery partition, it should be about 16 GB. Otherwise, an 8 GB flash drive is large enough.

Here are the steps to create the recovery drive:

1. Plug in a USB flash drive. Know that the entire drive will be formatted and everything on the drive will be lost.

2. Open **Control Panel** in icon view, and click **Recovery**. In the Recovery window that appears (see Figure 3-19), click **Create a recovery drive**. Respond to the UAC box.

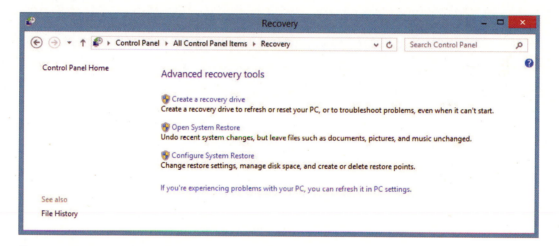

Figure 3-19 Use the Recovery window in Control Panel to create a recovery drive
Used with permission from Microsoft Corporation

3. The Recovery Drive dialog box appears (see Figure 3-20). If the computer doesn't have a recovery partition, the checkbox on this dialog box is gray and not available. If the computer has a recovery partition, the checkbox is available, and you can check it to copy the recovery partition to the recovery drive. Click **Next** to continue.

4. A list of installed drives appears (see Figure 3-21). Make certain you select the USB flash drive because everything on the drive will be lost. Click **Next**. A message on the next screen warns you that everything on the drive will be deleted. Click **Create**. The drive is created, which takes some time. Then click **Finish**.

Be sure to label the flash drive well, and put it in a safe place. For example, you can put it in an envelope and label it "Recovery drive for 32-bit Windows 8 computer" and store it with the computer's documentation. How to use a recovery drive is covered later in the chapter.

 **Notes** If you copied the recovery partition to the drive and are short on hard drive space on the computer, you can use Disk Management to delete the recovery partition to free up some space and then expand the Windows volume.

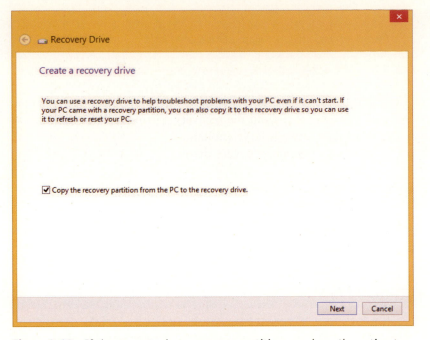

Figure 3-20   If the computer has a recovery partition, you have the option to
copy it to the recovery drive
Used with permission from Microsoft Corporation

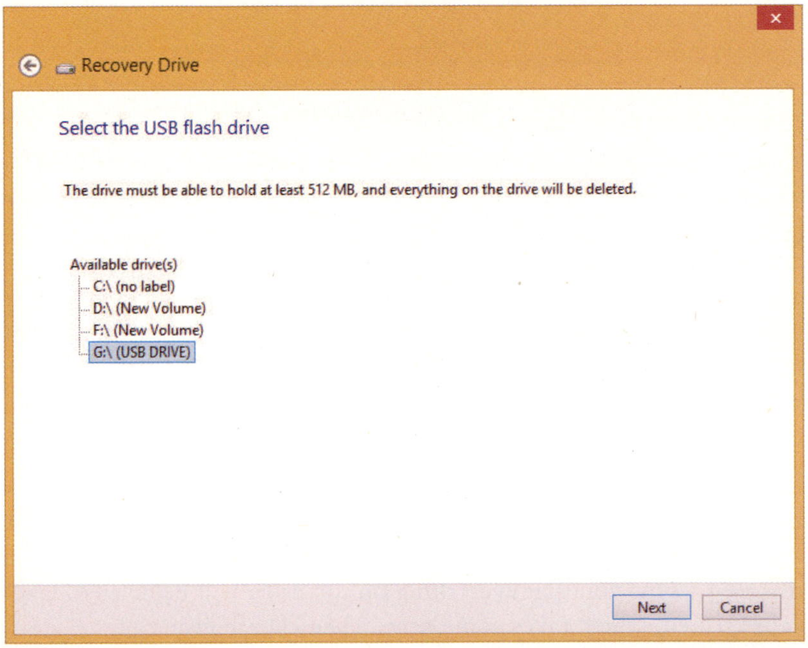

Figure 3-21   Select the USB flash drive that will become the recovery drive
Used with permission from Microsoft Corporation

PROTECT AGAINST MALWARE

As with any OS, the three most important things you can do to protect a system
against malware are to run antivirus software, maintain Windows updates, and secure
the network connection. You learned how to secure network connections in Chapter 2.
Next let's take a look at how to verify Windows Defender settings and Windows
Update settings.

WINDOWS DEFENDER

Windows 8 comes with a new Windows Defender that protects the system against viruses, adware, spyware, and other types of malware. Windows Defender runs by default and will not run if other antivirus software is running. To verify Windows Defender settings, go to the Start screen and open Windows Defender. (On the Start screen, start typing **Windows Defender**, and then click **Windows Defender** in the list of apps that appears.) The Windows Defender window appears on the desktop (see Figure 3-22). If real-time protection is not on, you can turn it on using the Settings tab.

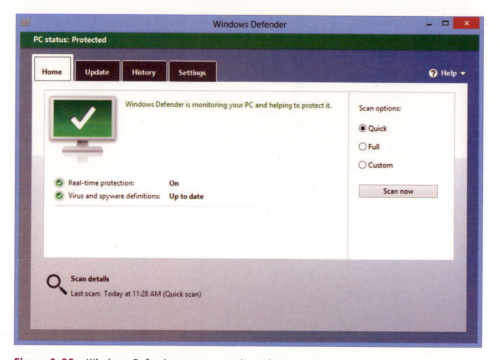

Figure 3-22 Windows Defender protects against viruses, spyware, and other malware
Used with permission from Microsoft Corporation

WINDOWS UPDATES

Recall that by default, Windows 8 automatically downloads and installs important updates daily at 3:00 AM. (Windows 8.1 installs updates at 2:00 AM.) Windows offers a way for end users to quickly check the status of updates: Open the **Settings** charm, click **Change PC settings**, click **Update and recovery**, and click **Windows Update**. Figure 3-23 shows a situation where there are no pending updates to be installed.

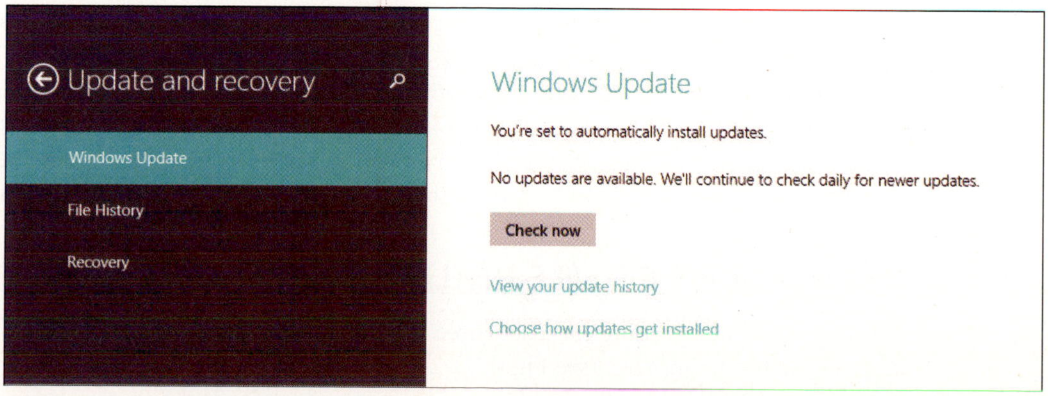

Figure 3-23 Windows Update screen shows the status of pending updates
Used with permission from Microsoft Corporation

You can change update settings using the link on this screen, but for more control over these settings, open the Windows Update window on the desktop. First open the **System** window (press **Win+X** and click **System**). In the System window, click **Windows Update**. In the Windows Update window (see Figure 3-24), you can drill down to see details about updates, install updates, and change update settings as is done in Windows 7.

Figure 3-24   Manage updates and update settings
Used with permission from Microsoft Corporation

Now let's turn our attention to Windows 8 troubleshooting tools.

TOOLS FOR TROUBLESHOOTING WINDOWS 8

The purpose of this part of the chapter is to show you how to use the troubleshooting tools new to Windows 8. If you want a complete discussion of how to troubleshoot a computer problem, see the main textbooks that accompany this Windows 8 book.

> **? To Learn More**   To learn more about troubleshooting Windows and applications, see Chapters 12 and 14 in *A+ Guide to Managing and Maintaining Your PC, 8th Edition*, or Chapters 5 and 6 of *A+ Guide to Software, 6th Edition*.

Your primary tools for solving problems after Windows starts include the Action Center, Event Viewer, Device Manager, and Task Manager. Except for Task Manager, these tools haven't changed much from Windows 7 to Windows 8. However, Windows 8 has quite a few changes for solving problems that occur at startup. Let's step through these tools and see how they work and also take note of Windows 7 tools that are missing in Windows 8. The diagram in Figure 3-25 can help you organize in your mind the various ways to boot the system and the menus and tools available to you depending on how you boot the system.

Basically, to fix a Windows problem, you can restart, repair, restore, refresh, and reset the system from within Windows or from other bootable media. Let's get started with the details.

USE WINDOWS 8'S SELF-HEALING FEATURE

If you restart the computer at least three times within a few minutes, Windows 8 automatically launches diagnostics (see Figure 3-26) and takes you through steps to attempt to repair the system. Sometimes a few restarts is all you need to do. If the system hangs while diagnosing and repairing, try another restart, which may fix the problem.

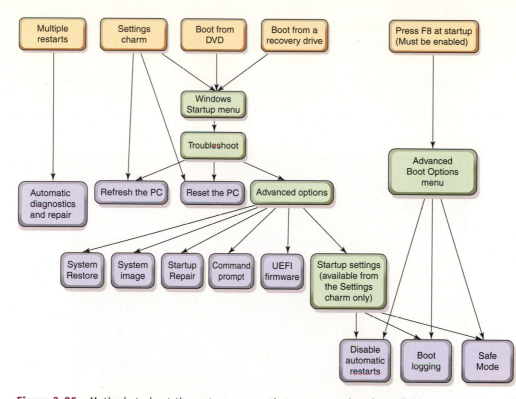

Figure 3-25 Methods to boot the system, menus that appear, and tools available on menus used to troubleshoot startup problems
Copyright © 2015 Cengage Learning

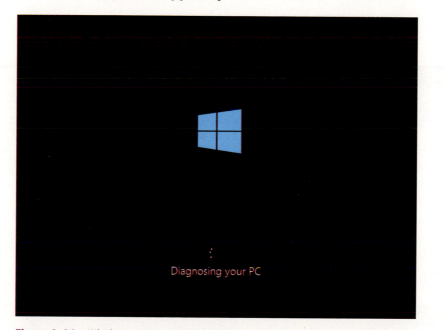

Figure 3-26 Windows automatically launches diagnostic procedures after the third restart within a few minutes
Used with permission from Microsoft Corporation

LAUNCH ADVANCED STARTUP FROM WITHIN WINDOWS

If you can load Windows, you can restart it in advanced startup mode, which includes repair, restore, refresh, reset, and other useful tools for troubleshooting. First use the **Settings** charm to open the **PC settings** screen, and click **Update and recovery**. Then click **Recovery**. Click **Restart now** under *Advanced startup* (refer back to Figure 3-12).

Windows restarts and launches Windows RE. The first screen provided by Windows RE is called the Windows Startup Menu and is shown in Figure 3-27.

> 📝 **Notes** You must be signed in to Windows 8 with an administrator account to see all the options on the Recovery pane that are shown in Figure 3-12.

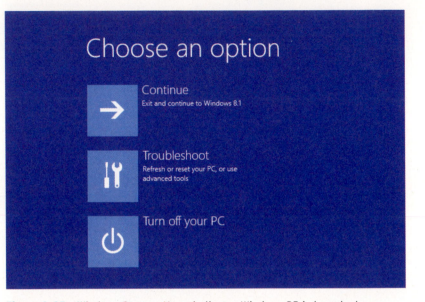

Figure 3-27 Windows Startup Menu indicates Windows RE is launched
Used with permission from Microsoft Corporation

> 📝 **Notes** Depending on the situation, you might see a fourth option on the Windows Startup Menu, which is *Use a device*. Select this option to restart the computer and boot from a USB drive, network connection, or Windows setup DVD.

When you click **Troubleshoot,** the Troubleshoot screen in Figure 3-28 appears. Using this screen, you can refresh or reset the computer or move on to advanced options. Before you do a refresh or reset, first go to the Advanced options and try a startup repair.

Click **Advanced options** to see the Advanced options screen (see Figure 3-29). Here you can perform a system restore (apply a restore point), use a system image to recover the system, change startup settings, perform a startup repair (similar to the Windows 7 Startup Repair process), and get to a command prompt.

> 📝 **Notes** Depending on the situation, you might see a sixth option on the Advanced options screen, which is UEFI Firmware Settings. Use this option to change settings in a computer's UEFI firmware.

If a critical Windows setting is a problem, click **Startup Settings** to view the Startup Settings screen (see Figure 3-30). Click **Restart.** Another Startup Settings screen shown in Figure 3-31 appears.

Use function keys F1 through F9 to make selections on this screen. All the selections here were available on the Advanced Boot Options menu in Windows 7 except *8) Disable*

Figure 3-28 Windows RE offers refresh and reset options to solve a computer
problem
Used with permission from Microsoft Corporation

Figure 3-29 More advanced tools for solving startup problems
Used with permission from Microsoft Corporation

early launch anti-malware protection. This new feature of Windows 8 allows antivirus
software to launch a driver before any third-party drivers are launched so it can scan
these drivers for malware. Unless you're sure a driver is the problem, don't disable this
security feature.

> **? To Learn More** To learn more about the options available on the Startup Settings screen that are
> also available in Windows 7, start at page 667 of Chapter 14 in *A+ Guide to Managing and Maintaining
> Your PC, 8th edition*, or page 265 of Chapter 6 in *A+ Guide to Software, 6th edition*.

3

Figure 3-30   Restart the computer to get to more advanced troubleshooting tools
Used with permission from Microsoft Corporation

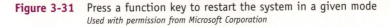

Figure 3-31   Press a function key to restart the system in a given mode
Used with permission from Microsoft Corporation

You can press F4 to launch Safe Mode. After you sign in to Windows, the Safe Mode desktop appears (see Figure 3-32). Launching Safe Mode and then restarting the system can sometimes solve a startup problem. However, you can also go to the Start screen in Safe Mode to launch antivirus software to scan the system for malware. You can also use the Quick Launch menu to open Event Viewer to find events helpful in troubleshooting the system, run the System File Checker command (`sfc /scannow`) to restore system files, and perform other troubleshooting tasks.

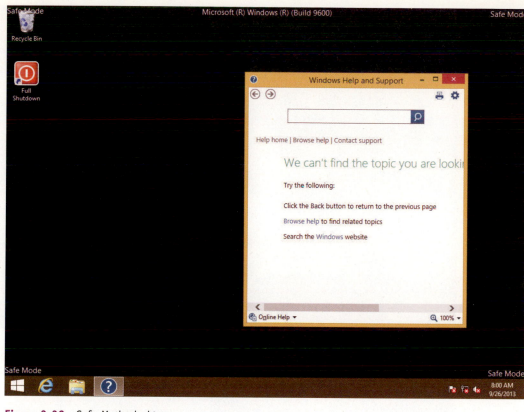

Figure 3-32 Safe Mode desktop
Used with permission from Microsoft Corporation

When you press F10 on the Startup Settings screen, the next screen allows you to launch the recovery environment (Windows RE), and you are taken back to the Windows Startup Menu screen shown previously in Figure 3-27.

BOOT FROM THE WINDOWS SETUP DVD

If Windows refuses to load, you need to boot the system from another bootable medium. One option is to use the Windows setup DVD. To boot from the optical drive, you might need to first go into BIOS setup and change the boot priority order.

When you first boot from the DVD, the Windows Setup window appears. Make your selections of language and keyboard layout, and click **Next**. On the next screen (see Figure 3-33), click **Repair your computer**. The Windows Startup Menu appears (refer back to Figure 3-27). You're now in Windows RE and can use all the screens and tools just discussed except the Startup Settings option, which is missing on the Advanced options screen when you boot from a medium other than the Windows volume (refer back to Figure 3-29).

BOOT FROM A RECOVERY DRIVE

If you don't have the Windows setup DVD handy or the computer does not have an optical drive, you can use a recovery drive to boot the system. You first might need to change the boot priority order in BIOS setup to boot to a USB device.

When you boot from a recovery drive, the first screen you see is the *Choose your keyboard layout* screen shown in Figure 3-34. Click **US** or your keyboard layout. Then Windows RE launches, and the Windows Startup Menu screen appears (refer back to Figure 3-27). You have all the troubleshooting tools available here except the Startup Settings option on the Advanced options screen is missing (refer back to Figure 3-29).

Figure 3-33 Use the Windows setup DVD to launch Windows RE
Used with permission from Microsoft Corporation

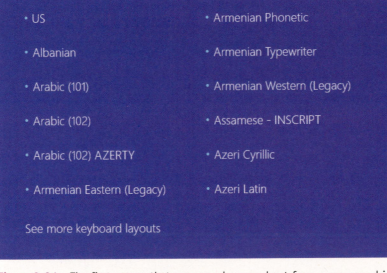

Figure 3-34 The first screen that appears when you boot from a recovery drive
Used with permission from Microsoft Corporation

BOOT TO THE ADVANCED BOOT OPTIONS MENU

Recall that Windows 7 allows you to press F8 to launch the Advanced Boot Options menu from the hard drive so you can launch Safe Mode, disable automatic restarts, and use other troubleshooting tools. Sadly, most computer manufacturers have F8 disabled at startup for Windows 8. If you have access to a computer before a startup problem happens, you can manually enable the use of F8 at startup.

To make the change, you'll need an elevated command prompt window. One way to open the window is to press **Win+X**, click **Command Prompt (Admin)**, and respond to the UAC box. In the command prompt window, enter this command (see Figure 3-35):

bcdedit /set {default} bootmenupolicy legacy

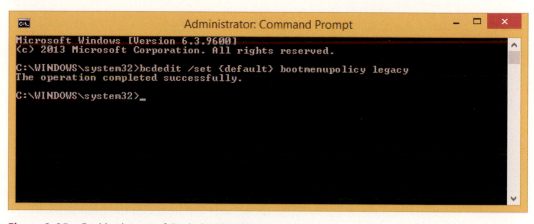

Figure 3-35 Enable the use of F8 during Windows startup
Used with permission from Microsoft Corporation

3

When Windows first starts to load, press **F8**, and the Advanced Boot Options menu appears (see Figure 3-36). Another sad fact: the Last Known Good Configuration option is missing from the menu. It looks like it's gone forever, having been replaced by system restore and a computer refresh.

```
                        Advanced Boot Options

Choose Advanced Options for: Windows 8.1
(Use the arrow keys to highlight your choice.)

    Repair Your Computer

    Safe Mode
    Safe Mode with Networking
    Safe Mode with Command Prompt

    Enable Boot Logging
    Enable low-resolution video
    Debugging Mode
    Disable automatic restart on system failure
    Disable Driver Signature Enforcement
    Disable Early Launch Anti-Malware Driver

    Start Windows Normally

Description: View a list of system recovery tools you can use to repair
            startup problems, run diagnostics, or restore your system.


ENTER=Choose                                              ESC=Cancel
```

Figure 3-36 Use the Advanced Boot Options menu to troubleshoot difficult startup problems
Used with permission from Microsoft Corporation

Later, if you want to disable the use of F8 at startup, open an elevated command prompt window and enter this command:

bcdedit /set {default} bootmenupolicy standard

> **?** **To Learn More** To learn more about the Advanced Boot Options menu in Windows 7, start at page 667 of Chapter 14 of *A+ Guide to Managing and Maintaining Your PC, 8th Edition*, and page 265 of Chapter 6 of *A+ Guide to Software, 6th Edition*.

SUMMARY OF TROUBLESHOOTING STRATEGIES

Now that you've seen the new Windows 8 troubleshooting tools, let's take a look at strategies for using them. Here's a list of what to do when:

1. Before anything goes wrong, take time to make a custom refresh image of the system after you've finished installing Windows, hardware, and applications and have user settings the way you want them. Save the image to the hard drive so it's easy for an end user to get to it when needed. You can also copy it to a network drive, external drive, or some other safe location.

2. Show every user you support how to use File History to back up their personal data and how to restore files from backups. Don't forget to ask the user to practice restoring a file or folder so he or she is comfortable with recovering lost data.

3. When troubleshooting a startup problem, follow procedures to interview the user, back up important data or verify you have current backups, research and identify any error messages, and determine what has just changed that might be the source of the problem. These troubleshooting skills work about the same way no matter which OS you're supporting.

> **?** **To Learn More** To learn more about troubleshooting Windows startup problems, see Chapter 14 in *A+ Guide to Managing and Maintaining Your PC, 8th edition*, or Chapter 6 in *A+ Guide to Software, 6th edition*.

4. When troubleshooting an unknown startup problem in Windows 8, use these tools, which are listed in the least intrusive order:

   a. *Restart:* Restart the system several times in succession and let Windows attempt to fix its own problems.

   b. *Repair:* Use the Startup Repair option on the Advanced options screen (refer to Figure 3-29).

   c. *Restore:* Use System Restore on the Advanced options screen.

   d. *Refresh:* Use the *Refresh your PC* option on the Troubleshoot screen (refer to Figure 3-28). This is the time to use the custom refresh image you made earlier.

   e. *Reset:* Use the *Reset your PC* option on the Troubleshoot screen. Basically, at this point, you've decided to completely start over with a fresh installation of Windows 8.

>> CHAPTER SUMMARY

Maintaining Windows 8

◢ The folder structure of Windows 8 is the same as that of previous Windows operating systems

◢ Press **Win+X** to open the Quick Launch menu where you can get to many tools for maintaining and troubleshooting Windows

◢ In Windows 8, the Startup tab of Task Manager is used to manage startup processes rather than the System Configuration utility that was used with previous Windows operating systems

◢ Windows 8 supports several tools for making backups of data and/or system files including restore points, File History, creating a recovery drive, and tools for resetting or refreshing Windows and making a custom refresh image

◢ File History backs up user data and is easy for end users to use

◢ Resetting a computer involves reinstalling Windows; all applications, data, and user settings are lost

◢ Refreshing a computer reinstalls Windows; data, user settings, and Windows 8 apps are backed up and then restored after the Windows installation. Desktop applications are lost unless a custom refresh image is used.

◢ Custom refresh images are intended to replace Windows 7 system images and are created and managed using the `recimg` command

◢ The major disadvantage of a custom refresh image over a Windows 7 system image is that the image cannot receive incremental changes

◢ You can create a recovery drive on a USB flash drive to repair the system when the Windows setup DVD is not available or the system doesn't have an optical drive

◢ If a computer has a recovery partition, that partition can be stored on a recovery drive

◢ Windows Defender is embedded in Windows 8 and protects against viruses, adware, spyware, and other malware. It is automatically disabled when other antivirus software is installed.

◢ By default, Windows 8 automatically downloads and installs important updates daily at 3:00 AM, and Windows 8.1 installs updates at 2:00 AM

Tools for Troubleshooting Windows 8

◢ Troubleshooting techniques to solve startup problems in Windows 8 include restarting, repairing, restoring, refreshing, and resetting the computer. Each technique in the list is more drastic and makes more changes to the system than the previous one.

◢ The restore, refresh, and reset procedures can be launched from within Windows or, when you cannot start Windows, the procedures can be launched from the Windows setup DVD or a recovery drive

◢ You can use the bcdedit command to change a default setting to cause Windows to launch the Advanced Boot Options menu when you press F8 at startup. This menu can be used to access advanced troubleshooting tools.

◢ The Last Known Good Configuration option available in previous Windows operating systems is not available in Windows 8

3

>> KEY TERMS

active recovery image – The custom refresh image that is registered with the system to be used during a refresh of Windows. The `recimg` command is used to set the active recovery image.

custom refresh image – An image of the Windows volume stored in a single file named CustomRefresh.wim. The image is created using the `recimg` command and used by the refresh procedure to reimage the volume.

File History – A backup tool new to Windows 8 used to back up and restore personal data folders and files to a specified drive. By default, backups are done hourly. File History can also be used to create a system image.

recovery drive – A bootable USB flash drive used to launch Windows RE. If a computer has a recovery partition, the partition can be copied to the recovery drive.

refresh Windows – A process that backs up user settings, data files, and Windows 8 apps, and then formats the Windows volume, reinstalls Windows, and restores what it backed up. Refresh can use a custom refresh image if one is available.

reset Windows – A process that formats the Windows volume and reinstalls Windows. If a recovery partition is present, it's used to reinstall Windows and return the system to the factory state.

>> REVIEWING THE BASICS

1. Which tab on the Task Manager window reports the system resources that a particular program is using?

2. Which tab on the Task Manager window is used to disable or enable processes that launch at startup?

3. Which tab on the Task Manager window can you use to launch Resource Monitor?

4. How do you turn a live tile off?

5. Which Windows tool is used to back up a user's personal data?

6. Which procedure causes user data and settings to be lost, refreshing Windows or resetting Windows?

7. Which Windows 8 tool is similar to and replaces a Windows 7 system repair disc?

8. By default, how often does File History back up files?

9. When you refresh Windows, where is the old installation of Windows stored?

10. If a computer has an active recovery image and a recovery partition, which one is used during a refresh of Windows?

11. How do you open an elevated command prompt window?

12. What is the command to create a custom refresh image and store the image in the C:\CustomImages folder?

13. What is the command to deregister the current active recovery image?

14. What is the file name and extension of a custom refresh image?

15. When is the best time to create a custom refresh image?

16. Which charm on the charms bar is used to refresh or reset a computer?

17. Which link in the Control Panel window is used to create a recovery drive?

18. When other antivirus software is running on a computer, can you also run Windows Defender?

19. List the steps to restart a computer in advanced startup mode to display the Windows Startup Menu used to troubleshoot a system.

20. What command line command can you use to cause Windows 8 to launch the Advanced Boot Options menu when you press F8 at startup?

>> THINKING CRITICALLY

1. Suppose you are about to donate a Windows 8 computer to a school. What should you do before the computer goes out the door?

a. Delete the Windows folder, and then perform a Windows 8 upgrade.

b. Copy all your data to an external storage device, and then refresh Windows.

c. Copy all your data to an external storage device, and then reset Windows.

d. Delete all your data on the hard drive, and then refresh Windows.

2. Which reasons might cause a custom refresh image to not be used when you refresh Windows? Select all that apply.

a. When the image was made months before you refresh Windows

b. When the image has been deregistered in the system

c. When another custom refresh image was made after this one

d. When the image was made on a different computer than the one being refreshed

3. How does Windows let you know that desktop applications were lost during a refresh?

a. Desktop apps are never lost during a refresh.

b. The lost desktop apps are stored in the Desktop.old folder.

c. A list of lost desktop apps is stored in the Removed Apps.html file on the desktop.

d. A list of lost desktop apps is stored in the Removed Apps.txt file on the desktop.

4. Which option on the Advanced options screen is available only when you restart the computer in advanced startup mode rather than from bootable media such as the Windows setup DVD?

a. System Restore

b. System Image Recovery

c. Startup Repair

d. Command Prompt

e. Startup Settings

>> HANDS-ON PROJECTS

PROJECT 3-1: Use File History

Follow these steps to learn to use File History:

1. Plug in a USB flash drive to be used as your backup storage device.

2. Put a document file in your Documents library on the hard drive.

3. Turn on File History to use the USB flash drive for backups. The backup should run immediately.

4. Make a change to the document, and run the backup again. Make a second change to the document, and run the backup a third time. Then delete the document from the Documents library.

5. Use File History to restore the last version of the file to the Documents folder. Now restore the original version of the file to the Documents folder.

6. Use File Explorer to examine your USB flash drive. What is the name of the folder that holds the backups made by File History? How many versions of the backed-up document are on your flash drive?

PROJECT 3-2: Create and Use a Custom Refresh Image

Do the following to practice using a custom refresh image:

1. Use the `recimg` command to create a custom refresh image. Where did you store the image?

2. Download and install a free app from the Windows Store.

3. Change the background picture of the Start screen.

4. Create a new file in your Documents library.

5. Go to **get.adobe.com/reader**, and download and install Adobe Reader. The reader installs on the Windows desktop.

6. Refresh Windows using the custom refresh image you created in Step 1. Which of the changes you made to Windows in Steps 2 through 5 are still in effect after the refresh and which are lost?

PROJECT 3-3: Boot to the Advanced Boot Options Menu

Following directions given in the chapter, use the `bcdedit` command to enable using the F8 key at startup. Restart the system, and press **F8** to verify you can launch the Advanced Boot Options menu at startup. Then restart Windows normally. Finally, use the `bcdedit` command again to disable using the F8 key at startup.

PROJECT 3-4: Create and Use a Recovery Drive

You'll need a USB flash drive with at least 8 GB storage capacity to do this project. Everything on the drive will be lost. Follow directions in the chapter to create a recovery drive using the flash drive. How much space on the drive is used by the recovery drive? Boot from the recovery drive, and verify you can access the troubleshooting screens discussed in the chapter.

> 📝 **Notes** To boot from a USB device, you might need to go into BIOS setup and change the boot priority order. Also know that some computers don't offer the option to boot from a USB device. If your computer does, you'll see USB listed as an option in the boot priority order in BIOS setup.

PROJECT 3-5: Find Windows Utilities

The following table lists some important Windows utilities used to support and troubleshoot a system. Fill in the right side of the table with how to open the utility and the file name and path of each utility. (Hint: You can use File Explorer or Search to locate files.)

Utility	How to Open	File Name and Path
Task Manager		
System Configuration Utility		
Services Console		
Computer Management		
Microsoft Management Console		
Event Viewer		
Resource Monitor		
Registry Editor		

>> REAL PROBLEMS, REAL SOLUTIONS

REAL PROBLEM 3-1: Perform a Clean Boot

When troubleshooting Windows problems, you might want to perform a clean boot to eliminate processes and services from launching at startup that might be the source of the problem or be causing a conflict with other programs. For more details about performing a clean boot, see the Microsoft knowledge base article 929135 at support.microsoft.com/kb/929135. Do the following to practice performing a clean boot:

1. Use Task Manager to disable all startup processes. Use the System Configuration utility to disable all non-Microsoft services that launch at startup.

2. Restart the computer. Note any changes or error messages you see during startup.

3. Return the startup process to start as usual. Restart the computer to verify that all works as it should.

REAL PROBLEM 3-2: Use NTFS Permissions to Share Files and Folders

When learning to support a new edition of Windows, know that your skills supporting previous editions will not go to waste. This book assumes you already know how to support Windows 7. Apply these Windows 7 skills to set up NTFS permissions and share permissions to share files and folders between two computers on a local network. In doing so, you'll see that Windows 7 and Windows 8 have much in common. Using two Windows 8 computers, do the following. As you work, write down each step you take in a log:

> **Notes** If you are working alone with only one computer, you can use two virtual machines installed in Client Hyper-V on your computer to do this Real Problem.

1. On Computer 1 and Computer 2, set the network security to Private.

2. On Computer 1, sign in as an administrator and create two folders: C:\Financial and C:\Medical. Put a text file in each folder.

3. On Computer 2, create three new standard user accounts: John, Mary, and Larry.

4. Set up NTFS permissions, and share permissions so the following is true:

   ▴ When John is signed on to Computer 2, he can read and write to the Financial and Medical folders on Computer 1

   ▴ When Mary and Larry are signed on to Computer 2, they can read and write to the Medical folder, but they are not allowed access to the Financial folder on Computer 1

5. Be sure to test your permissions by signing in to Computer 2 using the John, Mary, and Larry accounts and making sure all works as it should.

6. Compare the log you kept of steps with the log kept by another student. Look for differences and note them.

> **?** **To Learn More**   The skills used in this problem where not covered in the chapter because they work fundamentally the same way in Windows 7 and Windows 8. To learn more about how to share files and folders on a network, start at page 835 in Chapter 17 of *A+ Guide to Managing and Maintaining Your PC, 8th edition*, or page 383 in Chapter 8 of *A+ Guide to Software, 6th edition*.

Labs for Chapter 1: Using Windows 8

Labs included in this chapter:

- **Lab A.1:** Install a Windows 8 App and Manage the Start Screen

- **Lab A.2:** Use Task Manager

- **Lab A.3:** Use a Microsoft Account and SkyDrive

- **Lab A.4:** Use the Mail and People Apps

Notes The figures and steps in these labs use Windows 8.1 Professional. If you are using a different edition of Windows 8, your screens and steps may differ slightly from those presented here.

Notes The instructions in these labs assume that you are using a mouse and keyboard. If you're using a touch screen, simply tap instead of click; press and hold instead of right-click; double-tap instead of double-click; and swipe to scroll the screen to the right or left.

LAB A.1 INSTALL A WINDOWS 8 APP AND MANAGE THE START SCREEN

OBJECTIVES

The goal of this lab is to familiarize you with Windows 8. After completing this lab, you will be able to:

▲ Use the Windows 8 Start screen

▲ Find apps and settings

▲ Shut down Windows 8

MATERIALS REQUIRED

This lab will require the following:

▲ Windows 8 operating system

▲ Internet access

LAB PREPARATION

Before the lab begins, the instructor or lab assistant needs to do the following:

▲ Verify that Windows starts with no errors

▲ Verify Internet access is available

ACTIVITY BACKGROUND

Windows 8 has a very different user interface than previous editions of Windows. It can feel a little awkward or clumsy at first, but with time and practice you will feel comfortable using the new user interface.

> **Notes** Windows 8 hides shortcuts and menus. You can access them by placing your pointer in the corners of the screen.

ESTIMATED COMPLETION TIME: 45 Minutes

Activity

Follow these steps to become familiar with the Start screen:

1. By default, when you start Windows 8 and sign in, you are automatically taken to the Start screen. Find your user name in the top right of the screen. Click your **user name** icon.

2. Click **Lock** to password protect your screen. Click the **screen** to access the sign-in screen. Sign in to your account.

3. The Start screen has tiles used to open commonly used programs. Click the **Desktop** tile to access the Windows desktop. In Windows 8, the desktop is itself considered an app. To toggle between the Start screen and the desktop, use one of two methods:

   ▲ Click the **Start** (Windows logo) button in the taskbar. This button is hidden in this same corner when you're on the Start screen.

   ▲ Press the **Win** key on your keyboard.

4. After you open the desktop, you can return to it from the Start screen using one of two methods:

   ◢ Click the **Desktop** tile on the Start screen.

   ◢ Move your mouse to the top left of the screen, and click the **desktop** thumbnail.

> 📄 **Notes** If more than one app is open, you can quickly view one of these apps by moving your mouse to the top-left corner of the screen and then move your mouse down the left side of the screen. Thumbnails of the open apps appear for you to choose the app you want to view.

5. The desktop is itself an app, and you close it as you would any app. To close an app, drag the top edge of the page to the bottom edge of the screen. Close the desktop, and return to the Start screen.

6. On the Start screen, move an app tile. To move a tile, click and drag a tile to a different location on the screen.

7. Not all the tiles are the same size. To change the size of the Mail tile, right-click the **Mail** tile, which opens the settings options for the tile.

> 📄 **Notes** When you right-click a tile, you can select multiple tiles to change their settings at the same time.

8. In the status bar at the bottom of the screen, click **Resize**. Choose a different size. Notice the size of the tile changes.

9. To open a program that does not have a tile on the Start screen, simply start typing the name of the program. To open the Paint program, on the Start screen, type **Paint**. The Search pane opens showing a list. Select the **Paint** program in the search results. The Paint program opens on the desktop.

10. Close the Paint program. Return to the **Start** screen.

11. You're looking for a cooking and recipes app, and your friend recommended Allrecipes. To search for and download a new app, click the **Store** tile. The Store app opens. In the search box, type **Allrecipes**. In the results, click the **Allrecipes** icon.

12. Click **Install** as shown in Figure A-1. When Windows is done installing the Allrecipes app, you'll see a notification. Close the Store app by dragging the top edge of the page down to the bottom of the screen.

13. If you do not see the Allrecipes tile on the Start screen when you scroll to the right and left, type **Allrecipes**. In the search results, right-click the **Allrecipes** tile, and select **Pin to Start**. Click the **Start** screen to close the search results pane.

14. Scroll to the right until you see the Allrecipes tile. Open the **Allrecipes** app. Close the Allrecipes app.

15. To uninstall the Allrecipes app, right-click the **Allrecipes** tile. Click **Uninstall** in the status bar that appears at the bottom of the screen. Click **Uninstall** again.

16. Access the **charms** bar by moving your mouse to the top- or bottom-right corner of the screen. You can access the charms bar from anywhere in Windows, and the items on the charms bar might change, depending on the situation. What are the items in the charms bar you see on the screen?

A

Figure A-1   The Store is used to install the Allrecipes app
Allrecipes.com

17. On the charms bar, click the **Settings** charm (gear icon), and then click **Personalize**. Change the Start screen background picture or colors. Click the **Start** screen to close the Personalize pane.

18. On the Start screen, click the **down arrow** near the bottom left of the screen. The Apps screen appears listing all apps installed on the computer. Click the **up arrow** to return to the Start screen.

19. There are two ways to shut down the system:

   ◢ Open the **charms** bar, and click the **Settings** charm. Click the **Power** button, and select **Shut down** to turn off your computer.

   ◢ Press **Win+X**, select **Shut down or sign out**, then click **Shut down**.

REVIEW QUESTIONS

1. How do you open the Windows desktop? How do you close the desktop?

   _____

   _____

2. How do you install an app that uses the Windows 8 interface? How do you uninstall a Windows 8 app?

   _____

   _____

3. How do you access the Apps screen?

   _____

   _____

4. How do you add a tile to the Start screen?

_____

_____

5. How do you sign out from the computer? How do you shut down the computer?

_____

_____

LAB A.2 USE TASK MANAGER

OBJECTIVES

The goal of this lab is to help you use Task Manager to examine your system. After completing this lab, you will be able to:

▲ Identify applications that are currently running

▲ Launch an application

▲ Display general system performance and process information in Task Manager

▲ Manage startup programs

MATERIALS REQUIRED

This lab requires the following:

▲ Windows 8 Professional operating system

▲ Account with administrative access

LAB PREPARATION

Before the lab begins, the instructor or lab assistant needs to do the following:

▲ Verify that Windows starts with no errors

ACTIVITY BACKGROUND

Task Manager is a useful tool that allows you to view usage information for system resources, observe system performance, and manage processes. In this lab, you use Task Manager to manage applications and observe system performance.

ESTIMATED COMPLETION TIME: 45 Minutes

Activity

This lab is divided into two parts. In the first part, you explore Task Manager. In the second part, you learn to use tools in Task Manager.

Part 1: Explore Task Manager

Follow these steps to explore Task Manager:

1. Sign in to Windows 8 using an administrator account.

A

2. Open **Task Manager** using one of five methods:

   ◣ Press **Ctrl+Alt+Del**, and click **Task Manager**.

   ◣ Press **Win+X**, and click **Task Manager** in the Quick Launch menu.

   ◣ Right-click the **Start** button in the bottom-left corner of the screen, and click **Task Manager** in the Quick Launch menu.

   ◣ On the Start screen, type **Task Manager**. Select **Task Manager** from the search results.

   ◣ On the desktop, right-click the taskbar, and select **Task Manager**.

3. The Task Manager window opens on the desktop. If you don't see tabs, click **More details** at the bottom of the window. Tabs on the Task Manager window include Processes, Performance, App history, Startup, Users, Details, and Services, as shown in Figure A-2. Using these tabs, you can find information about applications, processes, and programs running on the computer and information on system performance.

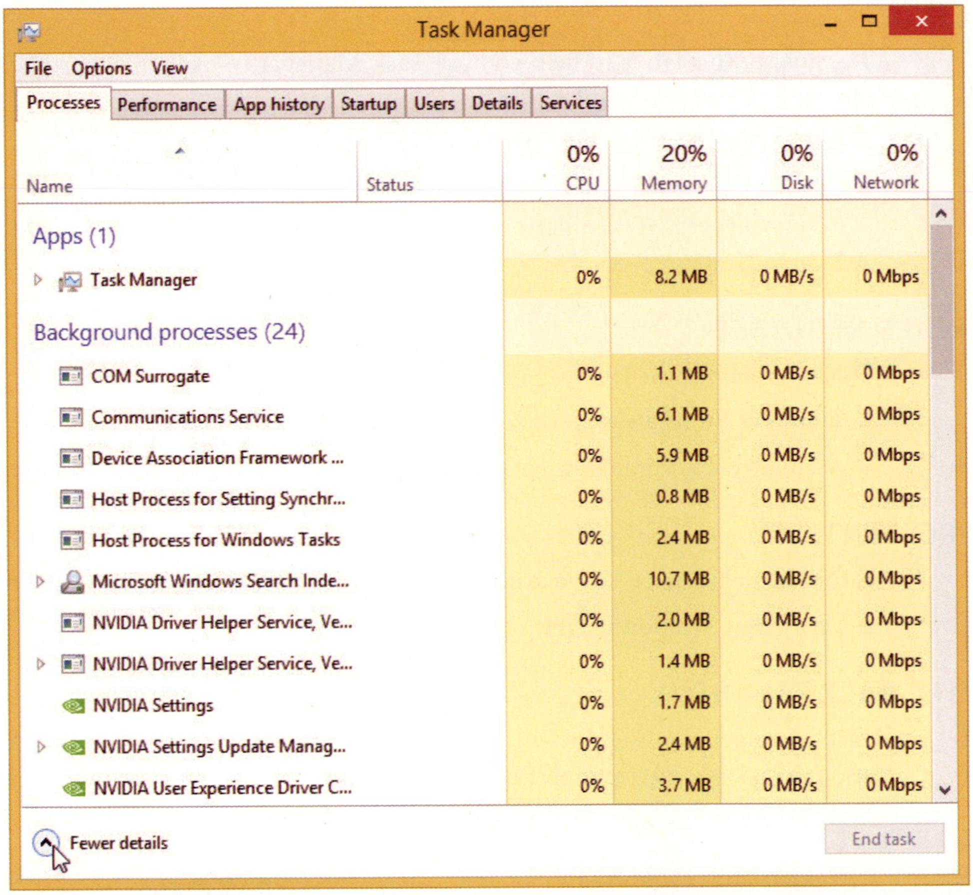

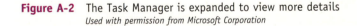

Figure A-2   The Task Manager is expanded to view more details
Used with permission from Microsoft Corporation

4. Click the **Details** tab. What information is viewed on the Details tab? (Hint: Look at the column headings.)

   _____

   _____

5. In the menu bar, click **File** and then **Run new task**. The Create new task dialog box opens, showing the last command entered if available.

6. In the Open box, delete any text already in the text box, and type **cmd**. "Cmd" is the command to open the command prompt window. Click **OK**. The command prompt window opens.

7. Now open an elevated command prompt window. List the steps you used.

   _____

   _____

   _____

8. Return to **Task Manager**. Find the two instances of cmd.exe on the Details tab in Task Manager. What is the status of each cmd.exe process?

   _____

9. Click the title bar of one of the command prompt windows, and drag the command prompt window so it overlaps the Task Manager window. The command prompt window is the active window and appears on top of Task Manager.

You can customize Task Manager to suit your preferences. Among other things, you can change the setting that keeps Task Manager on top of all other open windows and change the way information is displayed. To learn more about changing Task Manager settings, make sure one of the command prompt windows is still open and is on top of the Task Manager window. Follow these steps:

10. In Task Manager, click **Options** in the menu bar. Check **Always on top**, which keeps the Task Manager window on top of all other open windows. List the three options in the Options menu to manage the behavior of Task Manager:

    _____

    _____

    _____

11. Click the command prompt window. What happens?

    _____

12. In the Task Manager menu bar, click **View**. You can use the options on the Update speed submenu to change how quickly the information is updated. What are the four speed options?

    _____

13. Click somewhere else on Task Manager to close the menu view.

Follow these steps in Task Manager to observe process and performance information:

14. Click the **Processes** tab. This tab lists current processes in the Name column and displays information about each process, such as the percentage used by the CPU, Memory, Disk, and Network. Notice the Name column is divided by Apps, Background processes, and Windows processes.

15. Find the two instances of the command prompt windows. Click the **white arrow** to the left of each instance to expand the information about the process. How can you tell which instance is running with administrator privileges?

    _____

A

16. Scroll down and examine other processes. Which process is currently using the highest CPU and memory resources?

_____

_____

17. Now use the **Run new task** command in the File menu to observe the performance of your system. In the Run new task dialog box, type **cleanmgr.exe**, and click **OK**. If necessary, respond to the Disk Cleanup: Drive Selection dialog box that appears. (The box might be hidden behind the Task Manager window.)

18. As Disk Cleanup makes its calculations, watch the changes in the demand on the CPU on the Processes tab in the CPU column. What is the maximum amount of CPU resources that the cleanmgr.exe process used? (If Disk Cleanup ran too quickly for you to observe the columns in Task Manager, run it again.)

_____

19. Click the **Performance** tab, which displays CPU utilization, memory usage and composition, and disk active time and transfer rate for each installed hard drive. Bluetooth, Ethernet, and Wi-Fi throughput are displayed in bar graphs when available.

20. Click the **Open Resource Monitor** link at the bottom of the Performance tab. What are the four categories of information listed in the Resource Monitor window? Close the Resource Monitor window.

_____

Part 2: Use Task Manager tools

In addition to processes for user applications, the Processes and Details tabs in Task Manager display and allow you to end core Windows processes. Follow these steps to end a task:

> ⚡ **Caution**   Be careful about ending processes; ending a potentially essential process (which is one that other processes depend on) could have serious consequences. Because Disk Cleanup is not critical to core Windows functions, it's safe to end this process.

1. To end Disk Cleanup, select the **Details** tab. To make it easier to find the cleanmgr.exe task, click the **Name** column heading to sort the processes by name. The cleanmgr.exe task should be near the top of the list.

2. Select **cleanmgr.exe** in the list.

3. Use one of two methods to end the Disk Cleanup task:
   ◢ Right-click **cleanmgr.exe**, and click **End task**.
   ◢ Select **cleanmgr.exe** in the list of processes, and click the **End task** button in the bottom-right corner of the Task Manager window.

4. What message is displayed? Record it below, and then click **End process** in the Task Manager dialog box.

_____

_____

5. Close the two command prompt windows, or end the two cmd.exe tasks.

In previous versions of Windows, to manage startup programs, you accessed the System Configuration utility (Msconfig). In Windows 8, managing startup processes is done in Task Manager on the Startup tab.

Follow these steps to add the Notepad application to startup programs, and then use Task Manager to manage this startup program:

6. On the desktop, click the **File Explorer** icon. Use File Explorer to browse to **C:\Windows**.

7. Find the Notepad application. Right-click **Notepad**, and select **Create shortcut**. A warning box appears asking to create the shortcut on the desktop. Click **Yes**. A shortcut to the Notepad application is added to the desktop.

8. Now let's put the shortcut in a startup folder. In File Explorer, click **View** in the menu bar. The View ribbon appears. On the ribbon, place a checkmark next to **Hidden items** in the Show/hide group. Hidden folders and files appear.

9. Browse to **C:\Users*username*\AppData\Roaming\Microsoft\Windows\Start Menu\ Programs\Startup**.

10. Move the Notepad shortcut from the desktop to the Startup folder. Close all open windows.

11. Sign out of the computer, and sign in again. Open the **desktop**. Did the Notepad application open automatically?

   _____

12. Open **Task Manager**. Click the **Startup** tab. Notepad is now in the startup programs list.

13. Select **Notepad**, and click the **Disable** button at the bottom of the window. Now when you sign out and sign in again, will Notepad automatically open?

   _____

14. Sign out, and sign in again. Open the **desktop**. Did the Notepad application open automatically?

   _____

15. When you're finished, close all open windows.

REVIEW QUESTIONS

1. List five methods to launch Task Manager:

   _____

   _____

   _____

   _____

   _____

2. What are the steps to set Task Manager to always be on top of other windows on the desktop?

   _____

   _____

A

3. Why could it be dangerous to end a process with Task Manager? Give a detailed example.

_____

_____

_____

4. On the Performance tab in Task Manager, view the **Memory** information. The Task Manager indicates the number of memory slots used on the motherboard. Why might this information be useful to have available in Task Manager? How many slots are available on your system, and how many are currently used?

_____

_____

_____

_____

5. What is the path to the folder that contains startup programs for the currently logged on user?

_____

_____

6. Can you use Task Manager to add a new program to Windows startup? Can you use Task Manager to completely remove a program from the list of startup programs that appear on the Startup tab? How can you add a new program to the list of startup items?

_____

_____

_____

LAB A.3 USE A MICROSOFT ACCOUNT AND SKYDRIVE

OBJECTIVES

The goal of this lab is to set up a Microsoft account and use it to:

- ▲ Use a local account, a Microsoft account, and a SkyDrive
- ▲ Switch between a Microsoft account and a local account

MATERIALS REQUIRED

This lab requires the following:

- ▲ Windows 8 operating system
- ▲ Internet access

LAB PREPARATION

Before lab begins, the instructor or lab assistant needs to do the following:

- ▲ Verify that Windows starts with no errors
- ▲ Verify Internet access is available

ACTIVITY BACKGROUND

Windows 8 gives the user the option to log in with a Microsoft account. Using that account, the user can access his or her SkyDrive without entering a password. In this lab, you learn how all this works.

ESTIMATED COMPLETION TIME: 45–60 Minutes

Activity

1. What is the local account user name for your computer?

   _____

2. Do you have an existing Microsoft account using an Outlook.com, Hotmail.com, Live.com, or some other email address? If so, what is the email address associated with your Microsoft account?

   _____

Windows requires that you sign in with a Microsoft account before you can use the SkyDrive app. If you don't already have a Microsoft account, you'll have the opportunity to create one when you first attempt to open the app.

Part 1: Use a local account, a Microsoft account, and SkyDrive

1. Sign in with a local account.

2. On the Start screen, click the **SkyDrive** app. The SkyDrive app opens, but because you are signed in using a local account, SkyDrive cannot access your Microsoft account, which is required for SkyDrive. Click **Go to PC settings**.

3. Click **Connect to a Microsoft account**. The *Switch to a Microsoft account on this PC* screen appears. Enter your local account password. Click **Next**.

4. If you already have a Microsoft account, enter your sign-in information now. If you do not have a Microsoft account, click **Create a new account**.

   > **Notes** If you already have a Microsoft account, sign in to SkyDrive. When the SkyDrive app opens, skip to Step 6.

5. A Microsoft account is associated with an email address. You can use an existing email address or create a new one. Windows 8 apps work best if your Microsoft account uses an outlook.com, hotmail.com, or live.com email address. Create an email address that has an outlook.com, hotmail.com, or live.com ending. What is your new Microsoft account email address? (You might also want to write down your password in a safe place so you won't forget it.)

   _____

6. Complete the steps to set up your new Microsoft account, including creating the email address and password, security information, and finalizing the account.

7. You can skip the step to use the security code for now.

8. SkyDrive is introduced. Click **Next**.

A

9. Click **Switch**. Your local account has now been switched to a Microsoft account on the computer. Now, when you sign in to your computer, you use your Microsoft account information and *not* the local account sign-in information.

10. Close the SkyDrive app, and reopen it to verify you are signed in.

To add a document to the SkyDrive folder, we will first create one on the desktop. Follow these steps to upload a file to SkyDrive:

11. Open the **desktop**.

12. Right-click the **desktop**, and select **New, Text Document**. Rename the document **SkyDriveTest**.

13. Open the document, and type **This is my test document for SkyDrive in Windows 8**. Save the file, and close Notepad. Return to the **SkyDrive** app.

14. Right-click anywhere on the screen. Click the **Add items** icon in the status pane. A browsing screen opens.

15. With *This PC* showing, click the **Desktop** tile. (If *This PC* isn't showing, click the down arrow next to the title of the screen and select *This PC*.) Select the **SkyDriveTest** file, and then click the **Copy to SkyDrive** button. The file is added to your SkyDrive account.

16. View your document from your SkyDrive. Then return to the **Start** screen.

Part 2: Switch between a Microsoft account and a local account

Now let's disconnect the Microsoft account, and then reconnect the Microsoft account. Follow these steps to disconnect your Microsoft account from your local account:

1. From the Start screen, go to the **charms** bar, and click **Settings**. Click **Change PC settings**, and then click **Accounts** in the left pane.

2. On the Accounts screen, click **Disconnect** under your account name and email address as shown in Figure A-3. Confirm your current Microsoft password, and click **Next**.

Figure A-3   The Accounts page is used to connect or disconnect a Microsoft account to a local account
Used with permission from Microsoft Corporation

3. You cannot reuse your same local account user name; however, the user folders remain the same. Enter an alternate local account user name. Create the password and password hint. (You can reuse the local account password you used in the beginning of this lab.) Click **Next**.

4. You need to sign out and sign back in to complete the process. Click **Sign out and finish**.

5. Sign in to your local account. Do you think you can now use the SkyDrive app without entering your password again?

_____

6. Return to the **PC settings** screen, and reconnect to your Microsoft account.

7. Sign out and sign back in using your Microsoft account. Verify that you can use the SkyDrive app.

REVIEW QUESTIONS

1. Why can you not use the SkyDrive app while signed in using a local account?

_____

2. What are the three domain name endings offered when creating a new Microsoft account?

_____

3. How do you access the menu to add a new document to your SkyDrive?

_____

4. Why might you want to save files to SkyDrive instead of just saving to the local hard drive?

_____

5. List the steps to disconnect your Windows 8 local account from a Microsoft user account.

_____

_____

A

LAB A.4 USE THE MAIL AND PEOPLE APPS

OBJECTIVES

The goal of this lab is to use your Microsoft account to:

▲ Use the Mail app

▲ Use the People app to connect to other social accounts

MATERIALS REQUIRED

This lab requires the following:

▲ Windows 8 operating system

▲ Internet access

LAB PREPARATION

Before lab begins, the instructor or lab assistant needs to do the following:

▲ Verify that Windows starts with no errors

▲ Verify Internet access is available

ACTIVITY BACKGROUND

After you have set up your Microsoft account, the user can send and receive mail through the Mail app and connect to other contacts such as Facebook and Twitter using the People app. In this lab, you learn how all this works.

Estimated Completion Time: 45–60 Minutes

Activity

This activity is divided into two parts. In the first part, you learn to use the Mail app. In the second part, you learn to use the People app.

Part 1: Use the Mail app

Follow these steps to check if your Mail app is syncing with your Microsoft account:

1. Sign in using the Microsoft account you set up in Lab A.3.

2. Click the **Mail** tile. You don't need to add another account at this time.

3. Open the **charms** bar, and click **Settings**. On the Settings pane (see Figure A-4), click **Accounts**. On the Account pane, verify the email address is correct. If no email address is listed or the address is wrong, click **Add an account**, and follow the steps to set up your email using your Microsoft email. To close the Accounts pane, click somewhere else on the screen.

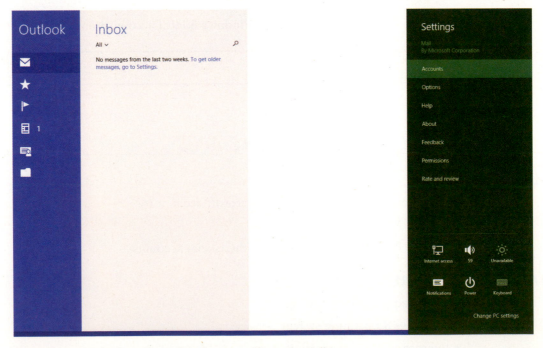

Figure A-4 The Settings charm lists items specific to the Mail app
Used with permission from Microsoft Corporation

4. By default, your Inbox for your email account is selected in the left pane. The list of emails in your Inbox appears in the middle pane. When you click an email, its contents appear in the right pane.

5. Send an email to yourself (or exchange emails with a classmate) to test the validity of the Mail app. Click the **New** button in the upper-right corner of the screen, and type a short message to yourself. Add a subject line, and click the **Send** button. The message quickly appears in your Inbox.

> **Notes** If you don't see the message, you might have typed the wrong email address. You can also try refreshing the sync with the mail server. Right-click somewhere in the Mail app. In the status pane, click **More**, then **Sync**.

6. There are a few ways to find the status bar where actions are available to handle your mail:

   ◢ Right-click the email in the middle pane.

   ◢ Place a checkmark by the email to select it.

   ◢ Click the three dots in the bottom-right corner of the screen.

   Notice a status bar appears at the bottom of the screen where you can print the message or mark it as Junk mail.

7. By default, mail is downloaded as it arrives. To see other options, open the **Settings** charm, and click **Accounts**. Then click your **email** address in the Accounts pane. What are the options for how often email is downloaded?

   _____

   _____

8. Close the Mail app.

Part 2: Use the People app

The People app is used to maintain all of your contacts, including those from Facebook, Outlook Mail, Google, and Twitter.

1. Return to the **Start** screen, and click the **People** app. Click **Connected to** in the bottom-right corner to access the Accounts menu.

2. Click **Add an account**.

3. Choose **Facebook** from the list. Review what else happens when you connect.

4. Click **Connect**. A Facebook login screen appears.

5. Enter your Facebook email account and password, then click **Log In**.

6. Microsoft asks to share your information, and then asks you a few other questions. Click **Okay** for each question to complete the connection of your People app to Facebook.

A

REVIEW QUESTIONS

1. What are the steps to add a second email account to the Mail app?

   _____

   _____

   _____

   _____

   _____

2. By default, not all your email is downloaded to the Mail app, but only email from the last 2 weeks. List the steps to have the Mail app download email from the last month.

   _____

   _____

   _____

3. What are the steps to add an Account in the People app?

   _____

   _____

   _____

   _____

4. Using the People app, what can you do when connected to your Facebook account?

   _____

   _____

   _____

LAB B

Labs for Chapter 2: Installing Windows 8

Labs included in this chapter:

- **Lab B.1:** Use the Windows 8 Upgrade Assistant

- **Lab B.2:** Perform a Clean Installation of Windows 8

- **Lab B.3:** Upgrade to Windows 8

- **Lab B.4:** Update to Windows 8.1 Using Windows Store

- **Lab B.5:** Use Client Hyper-V to Manage a VM

> **Notes** The instructions in these labs assume that you are using a mouse and keyboard. If you're using a touch screen, simply tap instead of click, press and hold instead of right-click, double-tap instead of double-click, and swipe to scroll the screen to the right or left.

LAB B.1 USE THE WINDOWS 8 UPGRADE ASSISTANT

OBJECTIVES

The goal of this lab is to help you decide if you should upgrade your computer to Windows 8. After completing this lab, you will be able to:

◢ Verify the compatibility of your computer, apps, and connected devices with Windows 8

MATERIALS REQUIRED

This lab will require the following:

◢ Windows 7 operating system

◢ Internet access

LAB PREPARATION

Before the lab begins, the instructor or lab assistant needs to do the following:

◢ Verify that Windows starts with no errors

◢ Verify that Internet access is available

ACTIVITY BACKGROUND

There are many reasons to upgrade your computer from Windows 7 to Windows 8. Maybe Windows 8 is a requirement for your job, or maybe you just want to see what all the fuss is about. No matter the reason you want to upgrade, you need to make sure your computer is compatible with the new OS before you perform the upgrade. Microsoft offers the Windows 8 Upgrade Assistant to scan your hardware, apps, and connected devices for compatibility for an upgrade assistant-download-online-faq. Before installing Windows 8, run the Upgrade Assistant from the Microsoft website.

ESTIMATED COMPLETION TIME: 30 Minutes

Activity

To download and run the Windows 8 Upgrade Assistant, follow these steps:

1. Open **Internet Explorer**, and browse to **windows.microsoft.com/en-us/windows-8/ upgrade-assistant-download-online-faq.** Review the information given about the Windows 8 Upgrade Assistant.

> **Notes** Websites change often. If you can't find the Upgrade Assistant at the link given, try this search string using Google.com: **Windows 8 Upgrade Assistant site:microsoft.com.**

2. Click **Download Windows 8 Upgrade Assistant.**

3. Internet Explorer pops up a notification asking if you want to run or save the file Windows8-UpgradeAssistant.exe. Select **Save,** and Internet Explorer automatically saves the file to the Downloads folder for the current user. When the download is complete, click **View Downloads.**

4. In the View Downloads window, click **Downloads** beside the filename you just downloaded. What is the path and filename (including file extension) of the downloaded file? What is the size of the file?

5. Close Internet Explorer and the View Downloads window.

6. To use the Upgrade Assistant, double-click the file you just downloaded to your Downloads folder. In the warning box, click **Run**.

7. When the scan is complete, click **See compatibility details** to review items scanned. Write down all items that need your review and all actions you take to resolve the compatibility issues.

_____

_____

_____

_____

_____

_____

_____

_____

_____

_____

8. To save the report, click **Save**. What is the path and filename (including file extension) of the downloaded file? What is the size of the file?

_____

9. Email the file to your instructor, or upload it to your online interface.

10. In the Windows 8 Upgrade Assistant, click **Next**.

11. With Windows settings, personal files, and apps selected, click **Next**.

12. The Windows 8 Upgrade Assistant displays the Windows 8 options for your computer. Which version or versions of Windows 8 can you upgrade your computer to?

_____

13. Click **Close**.

REVIEW QUESTIONS

1. Why is it a good idea to run the Windows 8 Upgrade Assistant before upgrading to Windows 8?

_____

2. What is the URL for the Windows 8 Upgrade Assistant?

_____

3. When preparing for an upgrade, is it more important to make sure you have Windows 8 drivers for your network adapter or your sound card? Explain your answer.

_____

_____

B

4. Describe the difficulty level of preparing your computer for an upgrade to Windows 8 and the problems you might encounter as you work.

_____

_____

_____

LAB B.2 PERFORM A CLEAN INSTALLATION OF WINDOWS 8

OBJECTIVES

The goal of this lab is to help you install Windows 8 without already having an OS installed on your computer. After completing this lab, you will be able to:

▲ Do a clean installation of Windows 8

MATERIALS REQUIRED

This lab will require the following:

▲ Windows 8 setup DVD or installation files at another location. Any edition of Windows 8 will work in this lab. If you are using an upgrade license of Windows 8, the edition of Windows 7 installed on the PC must qualify for the edition of Windows 8 you are using. Windows 7 Starter, Home Basic, and Home Premium can upgrade to Windows 8 or Windows 8 Pro. Windows 7 Professional and Ultimate can upgrade to Windows 8 Pro.

▲ Product key from Windows 8 package or downloaded from the Web

> 📝 **Notes** This lab gives steps for performing a clean installation of Windows 8. If you are using Windows 8.1, your steps might differ slightly.

LAB PREPARATION

Before the lab begins, the instructor or lab assistant needs to do the following:

▲ Verify that Windows starts with no errors

▲ Provide each student with access to the Windows 8 installation files and product key

▲ Verify that any necessary Windows 8 drivers are available

ACTIVITY BACKGROUND

When deciding to do a clean installation or upgrade to Windows 8, you need to consider the condition of your current system. If the Windows 7 system is giving trouble, performing a clean installation is a good idea so current problems don't follow you into the new installation. Also, you might do a clean installation if your computer does not already have an OS installed, such as on a new virtual machine.

ESTIMATED COMPLETION TIME: 60 Minutes

🔲 **Activity**

Follow these steps to perform a clean installation using a Windows 8 installation DVD:

1. Start up your computer and access BIOS setup. Change the boot sequence so the DVD-ROM is the first boot device.

2. Insert the Windows 8 DVD into the optical drive.

3. Shut down your computer, and start it up again.

4. You might be asked to press any key on your keyboard to boot from the DVD. The computer should boot the DVD and begin the installation process.

5. A Windows Setup box appears asking you to select your language, time and currency format, and keyboard input method. Make the appropriate selections. Click **Next**.

6. In the next Windows Setup box, click **Install now**.

7. A Windows Setup box asks for the product key that is used to activate Windows. Enter the product key for Windows 8, and click **Next**.

8. The license terms box appears. Check **I accept the license terms**, and click **Next**.

9. When prompted for the type of installation, select **Custom: Install Windows only (advanced)**.

10. In the next box, select a partition, and click **Next**. (If you need clarification at this point in the installation, ask your instructor for assistance.) The installation process begins, which can take several minutes. What is the size of the partition that will hold Windows 8?

_____

11. The computer might restart by itself several times as part of the installation process. If prompted to press any key to boot the CD or DVD, *ignore the message* because pressing any key will start the installation again from scratch.

12. The Personalize screen asks you to choose a screen color and type the PC name. Enter the PC name as assigned by your instructor. Click **Next**.

13. On the Settings window, click **Use express settings**.

14. You will set up a local account to sign in to Windows. On the *Sign in to your Microsoft account* window, click **Create a new account** from the options at the bottom of the screen, as shown in Figure B-1. Click **Sign in without a Microsoft account** to create a local

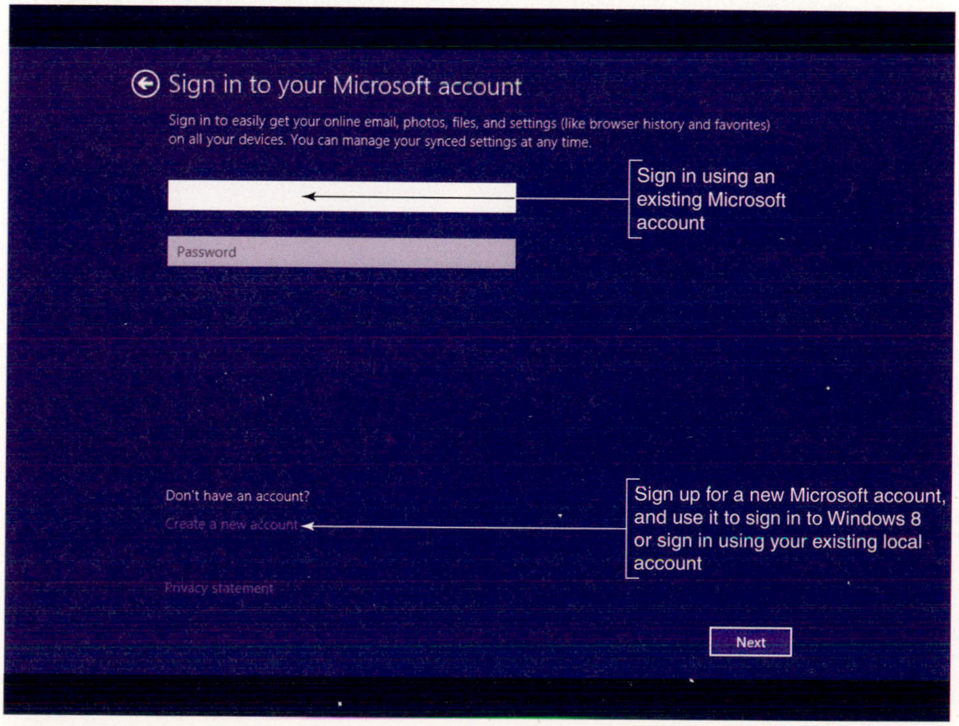

Figure B-1   Decide which account you will use to sign in to Windows 8
Used with permission from Microsoft Corporation

account. Type the user name, password in both boxes, and the password hint. Click **Finish**. So you do not forget your password, write the user name and password here:

_____

15. The computer takes a few minutes while Windows 8 finalizes settings, and then the Start screen appears. You are finished performing a clean installation of Windows 8.

16. Open **File Explorer** or the **Computer** window. How much space on the hard drive did the Windows 8 installation use?

_____

REVIEW QUESTIONS

1. Was the Windows 8 installation a success? If so, what did you find to be most challenging about the installation process?

_____

_____

2. When is a clean installation preferred over an upgrade to Windows 8?

_____

_____

_____

_____

3. In this lab, you created a local account to sign in to Windows. Was it necessary to be connected to the Internet to create the account? If you had created a Microsoft account to sign in to Windows, would it be necessary to be connected to the Internet to create the account?

_____

4. Why do you need to access BIOS setup before the installation process?

_____

_____

5. Did Windows automatically activate during the installation? How can you find out if Windows is activated?

_____

_____

LAB B.3 UPGRADE TO WINDOWS 8

OBJECTIVES

The goal of this lab is to help you upgrade to Windows 8. After completing this lab, you will be able to:

▲ Upgrade to Windows 8

MATERIALS REQUIRED

This lab will require the following:

▲ Windows 7 operating system

▲ Windows 8 setup DVD or installation files at another location. Any edition of Windows 8 will work in this lab so long as the edition of Windows 7 installed on the PC qualifies for the edition of Windows 8 you are using. Windows 7 Starter, Home Basic, and Home Premium can upgrade to Windows 8 or Windows 8 Pro. Windows 7 Professional and Ultimate can upgrade to Windows 8 Pro.

▲ Product key from Windows 8 package or available on the Web

> **Notes** You cannot perform an in-place upgrade from Windows 7 directly to Windows 8.1.

LAB PREPARATION

Before the lab begins, the instructor or lab assistant needs to do the following:

▲ Verify that Windows starts with no errors

▲ Provide each student with access to the Windows 8 installation files and product key

▲ Verify that any necessary Windows 8 drivers are available

ACTIVITY BACKGROUND

Performing an upgrade to Windows 8 takes less time than performing a clean installation of Windows 8. It also has the advantage that user preferences and settings are not lost and applications are left in working condition. If there isn't a reason for a clean install, an upgrade is recommended.

ESTIMATED COMPLETION TIME: 45 Minutes

Activity

The following steps are representative of a typical upgrade. Don't be alarmed if your experience differs slightly. Use your knowledge to solve any problems on your own, and ask your instructor for help if you get stuck. You might want to record any differences between these steps and your own experience. Also, record any decisions you make and any information you enter during the installation process.

Follow these steps to perform an in-place upgrade to Windows 8 when you're working with a Windows 8 setup DVD:

1. As with any upgrade installation, before you start the upgrade, do the following:

   a. Scan the system for malware using an updated version of antivirus software. When you're done, be sure to close the antivirus application so it's not running in the background.

   > **Notes** If you need help running antivirus software, refer to Lab C.2.

   b. Uninstall any applications or device drivers you don't intend to use in the new installation.

   c. Make sure your backups of important data are up to date, and then close any backup software running in the background.

B

2. Insert the Windows 8 setup DVD. If the setup program doesn't start automatically, open Windows Explorer, and double-click the setup program in the root of the DVD. (If you're not using a DVD to perform the upgrade, launch the setup program from wherever it is stored.)

3. Respond to the UAC box.

4. The setup program loads files, examines the system, and reports any problems it finds. If it finds the system meets minimum hardware requirements, setup asks permission to go online for updates. Make your selection, and click **Next**.

5. The next window requests the product key. Enter the product key, and click **Next**.

6. The product key is verified, and then the License terms window appears. Check **I accept the license terms**, and click **Accept**.

7. On the *Choose what to keep* screen, with **Keep Windows settings, personal files, and apps** selected, click **Next**.

8. On the next screen, verify the choices listed, and click **Install** to begin the installation.

9. During the installation, setup might restart the system several times. If prompted to press any key to boot into the CD or DVD, *ignore the message* because pressing any key will start the installation again from scratch.

10. The Personalize window asks you to choose a screen color. Click **Next**.

11. On the Settings window, click **Use express settings**.

12. On the next screen, enter the password for your local user account.

13. On the next screen, you are given the opportunity to enter a Microsoft account. To skip this step, click **Skip**. You can set up a Microsoft account later. The computer takes a few minutes while Windows 8 finalizes settings, then the Start screen appears. You are finished performing an upgrade installation of Windows 8.

REVIEW QUESTIONS

1. Was the Windows 8 installation a success? If so, what did you find to be most challenging about the upgrade process?

   _____

   _____

2. Using File Explorer, find out how much free space is on drive C. Also, how large is the Windows folder?

   _____

   _____

3. What is the size of the Windows.old folder? What is the purpose of this folder?

   _____

   _____

4. When performing a clean install of Windows, setup gives you the opportunity to create a user account and password during the installation process. Why do you think setup skipped this step in an upgrade installation?

   _____

LAB B.4 UPDATE TO WINDOWS 8.1 USING WINDOWS STORE

OBJECTIVES

The goal of this lab is to help you update to Windows 8.1. After completing this lab, you will be able to:

◢ Update to Windows 8.1 using the Windows Store

MATERIALS REQUIRED

This lab will require the following:

◢ Windows 8 operating system that does not have the Windows 8.1 update

◢ Internet access

LAB PREPARATION

Before the lab begins, the instructor or lab assistant needs to do the following:

◢ Verify that Windows starts with no errors

◢ Verify that Internet access is available

◢ Verify that any necessary Windows 8 drivers are available

ACTIVITY BACKGROUND

Windows 8.1 is offered as a free upgrade if you already have Windows 8 installed on your computer. The Windows 8.1 release works for any edition of Windows 8. To make sure you have the latest features of Windows 8, always install new releases of Windows 8 as they become available.

ESTIMATED COMPLETION TIME: 30 Minutes

Activity

Follow these steps to perform an update to Windows 8.1:

1. As with any update, before you start the update, do the following:

    a. In Windows 8, use the **System** window to check for updates and verify that all important updates are installed. If the KB2871389 updated is not installed, the Windows 8.1 update does not appear in the Windows Store.

    b. Scan the system for malware using an updated version of antivirus software. When you're done, be sure to close the antivirus application so it's not running in the background.

    Notes If you need help running antivirus software, refer to Lab C.2.

    c. Uninstall any applications or device drivers you don't intend to use after the update.

    d. Make sure your backups of important data are up to date, and then close any backup software running in the background.

2. To view which release of Windows is installed, press **Win+X**, and click **System**. The System window reports the release. Which release is installed? Is the installation a 32-bit or 64-bit installation?

B

3. Go to the **Start** screen, and open the **Store** app. Find and download the Windows 8.1 release. The process of installing Windows 8.1 is similar to installing Windows as an upgrade.

4. You must restart Windows, accept the license agreement, decide how settings are handled, and set up a user account or use an existing account. Sign in using a local account. To use a local account, when asked to sign in to your Microsoft account, click **Create a new account**. Then click **Sign in without a Microsoft account**.

REVIEW QUESTIONS

1. Was the Windows 8.1 update a success? If so, what did you find to be most challenging about the update process?

   _____

   _____

2. Why is it a good idea to scan your system for malware before performing an update?

   _____

   _____

3. Why do you not need the Windows 8 setup DVD or installation files to update to Windows 8.1?

   _____

   _____

4. Where do you locate the Windows 8.1 update?

   _____

LAB B.5 USE CLIENT HYPER-V TO MANAGE A VM

OBJECTIVES

The goal of this lab is to help you install and use virtual machines with Client Hyper-V in Windows 8 Pro. After completing this lab, you will be able to:

▲ Turn on Hyper-V in Windows 8 Pro

▲ Set up Hyper-V to allow a VM to connect to the network

▲ Create a VM using Hyper-V

▲ Use the VM in Hyper-V

MATERIALS REQUIRED

This lab will require the following:

▲ Windows 8 Professional 64-bit operating system

▲ Windows 8 setup DVD or installation files at another location

> 📝 **Notes** The steps in this lab use Windows 8.1 Professional. If you are using a different edition of Windows 8, your screens and steps may differ slightly from those presented here.

LAB PREPARATION

Before the lab begins, the instructor or lab assistant needs to do the following:

▲ Verify that Windows starts with no errors

▲ Provide each student with access to the Windows 8 installation files and product key

ACTIVITY BACKGROUND

If you need quick and easy access to more than one operating system or different configurations of the same operating system, a virtual machine is a handy tool to have. The virtual machine creates a computer within a computer, almost as if you are remote controlling a computer in a different location from a window on your desktop. Virtual machines are heavily used by IT support to replicate and resolve issues, test software, and learn about new operating systems.

> **Notes** Hyper-V will not work in Windows 8 Pro that is installed in a virtual machine. In other words, you can't use Hyper-V to create a VM within a VM. Also, you must have the 64-bit version of Windows 8 Pro installed to use Hyper-V.

ESTIMATED COMPLETION TIME: 45 Minutes

Activity

The steps to set up a VM using Windows 8 Pro are in three parts in this lab. In Part 1 you prepare Hyper-V to create a VM, and then you create the VM in Part 2. In Part 3 you manage and use the VM.

Part 1: Prepare Hyper-V using Windows 8 Pro

To configure Hyper-V in Windows 8 Pro, follow these steps:

1. For Hyper-V to work, hardware-assisted virtualization (HAV) must be enabled in BIOS setup. If you are not sure it is enabled, power down your computer, turn it on, go into BIOS setup, and make sure hardware-assisted virtualization is enabled. Also make sure that all subcategory items under HAV are enabled. Save your changes, exit BIOS setup, and allow the system to restart to Windows 8.

> **Notes** HAV might have a different name in the BIOS setup screens on your motherboard. Intel BIOS calls HAV Intel Virtualization Technology. AMD calls it AMD-V.

2. Open the **System** window. Which edition and version of Windows 8 is installed? If 64-bit Windows 8 Pro is not installed, don't continue with this lab.

3. Hyper-V is disabled in Windows 8 Pro by default. To turn it on, press **Win+X**. In the Quick Launch menu that appears, click **Programs and Features**.

4. Click **Turn Windows features on or off**. Place a check mark next to Hyper-V as shown in Figure B-2, and click **OK**.

B

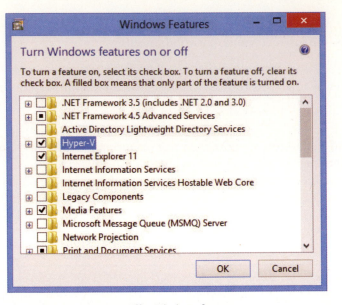

Figure B-2 Turn on or off a Windows feature
Used with permission from Microsoft Corporation

5. Windows applies the changes. Click **Restart now**, and sign in to the computer after it has restarted a couple of times.

6. To launch the Hyper-V Manager, go to the Start screen, and start typing **Hyper-V**, and then click the **Hyper-V Manager** tile. Alternately, you can click the Hyper-V Manager tile on the Start screen. The Hyper-V Manager window appears on the desktop.

7. In the Hyper-V Manager left pane, select the host computer.

8. To make sure your VMs have access to the network or the Internet, you need to first install a virtual switch in Hyper-V. To create a virtual switch, in the Actions pane on the right, click **Virtual Switch Manager**.

9. The Virtual Switch Manager dialog box appears. In the left pane, make sure **New virtual network switch** is selected. To bind the virtual switch to the physical network adapter so the VMs can access the physical network, select **External** in the left pane, and click **Create Virtual Switch**.

10. In the Virtual Switch Properties pane that appears, make sure **Allow management operating system to share this network adapter** is checked, and then click **Apply**. Click **Yes**, and the virtual switch is created. Click **OK** to close the Virtual Switch Manager.

Part 2: Create a VM using Hyper-V

To create a VM, follow these steps:

1. In the Actions pane, click **New**, and then click **Virtual Machine**. The New Virtual Machine Wizard launches. Click **Next**.

2. In the next dialog box, assign a name to the VM. Click **Next**. What is the name you assigned the VM?

_____

3. In the Specify Generation box, Generation 1 is selected. Click **Next**.

4. In the next box, set the amount of RAM for the VM as **4096 MB**. Check **Use Dynamic Memory for this virtual machine**. Click **Next** to continue.

5. In the Configure Networking box, in the drop-down options, select the new virtual switch you created earlier, and click **Next**.

6. In the Connect Virtual Hard Disk box, with **Create a virtual hard disk** selected, leave the default settings. Click **Next**.

7. Your instructor will provide access to operating system installation files. In the Installation Options box, decide how you will install an OS in the VM, and click **Next**. How are you planning to install an OS in the VM?

8. The last box shows a summary of your selections. Click **Finish** to create the VM. The new VM is listed in the Virtual Machines pane in the Hyper-V Manager window.

Part 3: Manage and use the VM

Follow these steps to configure and use the VM:

1. To manage the VM's virtual hardware, select the VM, and click **Settings** near the bottom of the Actions pane. The Settings box for the VM appears.

2. Explore the hardware listed in the left pane, and apply your settings in the right pane. Using the right pane, you can mount a physical CD or DVD to the drive or you can mount an ISO file.

3. To install an OS in the VM, you can boot the VM to the DVD drive, which is mounted to a physical setup DVD or to a bootable ISO file. To boot to the DVD drive, use the Settings box to verify the BIOS for the VM has the correct boot priority order. To view and change this setting, click **BIOS** in the left pane.

4. Click **OK** to close the Settings box. To start the VM, select it, and click **Start** in the Actions pane. The VM boots up, and you can then install an OS. Which OS are you installing?

5. A thumbnail of the VM appears in the bottom-middle pane of the Hyper-V Manager window. To see the VM in its own window, double-click the thumbnail as shown in Figure B-3.

Figure B-3 Windows 8 setup is running in the VM
Used with permission from Microsoft Corporation

B

6. Install the OS, and start up the operating system in the VM.

7. In the VM, open **IE** to confirm the VM has a good Internet connection.

8. Hyper-V allows you to close the application without shutting down virtual machines that are running in it. Close the VM window. Notice the state of the VM is listed as Running. How much memory is currently assigned to the VM?

_____

9. Close the Hyper-V Manager window and any other open Windows. Restart **Windows 8**.

10. After Windows restarts, sign in to Windows. On the Start screen, launch the **Hyper-V Manager**. What is the state of the VM you created? How much memory is currently assigned to the VM?

_____

11. Open the VM window, and use the VM to surf the Web. Finally, using the toolbar in the Virtual Machine Connection window, under *Action*, select **Shut Down**. Confirm your action by clicking **Shut Down** again. Now what is the state of the VM?

_____

12. Close all open windows.

REVIEW QUESTIONS

1. Were you able to successfully install the virtual machine using Hyper-V? If so, what did you find to be most challenging about the process?

_____

_____

2. Which edition and version of Windows 8 did you use during this lab and why?

_____

3. Why did you create a virtual switch?

_____

_____

_____

4. Why would you use dynamic memory with a virtual machine?

_____

5. When you close the Hyper-V application and have VMs running in it, what happens to the states of the VMs? What happens to the VM states when you open Hyper-V?

_____

_____

Labs for Chapter 3: Maintaining and Troubleshooting Windows 8

Labs included in this chapter:

- **Lab C.1:** Gather and Record System Information

- **Lab C.2:** Protect Against Malware

- **Lab C.3:** Use the Problem Steps Recorder

- **Lab C.4:** Explore Tools to Solve Windows 8 Startup Problems

- **Lab C.5:** Create and Use a Custom Refresh Image

- **Lab C.6:** Sabotage and Repair Windows 8

> 📝 **Notes** The figures and steps in these labs use Windows 8.1 Professional. If you are using a different edition of Windows 8, your screens and steps may differ slightly from those presented here.

> 📝 **Notes** The instructions in these labs assume that you are using a mouse and keyboard. If you're using a touch screen, simply tap instead of click; press and hold instead of right-click; double-tap instead of double-click; and swipe to scroll the screen to the right or left.

LAB C.1 GATHER AND RECORD SYSTEM INFORMATION

OBJECTIVES

The goal of this lab is to help document a system configuration. In this lab you use the operating system to determine how the system is configured. You also observe the condition of the system using a health report. After completing this lab, you will be able to:

▲ Gather system information using Windows tools

▲ Use available Windows tools to evaluate the condition of a system

MATERIALS REQUIRED

This lab requires the following:

▲ Windows 8 operating system

▲ Network connection

LAB PREPARATION

Before the lab begins, the instructor or lab assistant needs to do the following:

▲ Verify that Windows starts with no errors

▲ Verify that each computer is connected to the network

ACTIVITY BACKGROUND

This lab is done in two parts. In the first part of this lab, you identify the Windows configuration by using Windows tools. In Part 2 you learn an interesting shortcut to help you find several different ways to customize settings in Windows 8.

Activity

Part 1: Explore the system using Windows tools

The System Information window provides information about your system. Follow these steps to gather information about your system using the System Information window:

1. Open the Windows desktop. Press the **Win+X** keys or right-click the **Start** button in the taskbar to open the Quick Launch menu. Click **System**. The System window opens.

2. If necessary, expand this window so you can see all the information given. Using this information, fill in the following items.

   ▲ OS edition _____

   ▲ Processor _____

   ▲ Processor speed _____

   ▲ Installed memory (RAM) _____

   ▲ System type _____

   ▲ Computer name _____

   ▲ Workgroup _____

3. Close the System window.

The System Information utility provides additional information about hardware components and configuration of your system. Do the following to gather this information:

1. *System manufacturer and model:* To open the System Information utility, press **Win+X**, click **Run**, enter **Msinfo32.exe** in the Run box, and press **Enter**. The System Information window opens. On the System Summary page, find your system's manufacturer and model number and record them here:

   System Manufacturer: _____

   System Model: _____

2. *Drives:* Click the + sign next to the Components node on the navigation tree in the left pane. Click the + sign next to the Storage node, then click **Drives**. Record the following information:

Drive #1		Drive #2		Drive #3	
#1 Drive letter		#2 Drive letter		#3 Drive letter	
#1 Description		#2 Description		#3 Description	
#1 Size		#2 Size		#3 Size	
#1 Vol. name		#2 Vol. name		#3 Vol. name	
#1 Serial no.		#2 Serial no.		#3 Serial no.	

3. *Disks:* Click **Disks** in the navigation tree, and record the following information:

Disk #1		Disk #2	
#1 Manufacturer		#2 Manufacturer	
#1 Model		#2 Model	
#1 Partitions		#2 Partitions	
#1 Size		#2 Size	

4. Close the System Information window.

The Network screen offers information about your network connections. Follow these steps to gather information about your network connection:

1. On the charms bar, click the **Settings** charm. Then click **Change PC settings**.

2. Click **Network** in the left pane. Click to open your network connection. Record the following information:

   IP address: _____

   Physical address: _____

3. Close the Network Properties page.

Part 2: Try a cool shortcut for Windows 8

Windows 8 offers all kinds of settings to customize the Windows experience. The problem is that these settings can be hard to find sometimes. Follow these steps to create a shortcut to bring many settings all to one easy-to-locate icon.

1. On the desktop, create a new folder.

2. Rename this folder using this text (no spaces):
   Settings.{ED7BA470-8E54-465E-825C-99712043E01C}

C

3. The icon changes appearance. Double-click the new icon on your desktop, and explore the settings that are now all in this single location. The first category of settings is the Action Center, which has 17 items (see Figure C-1). How many categories of settings do you see in your Settings window?

_____

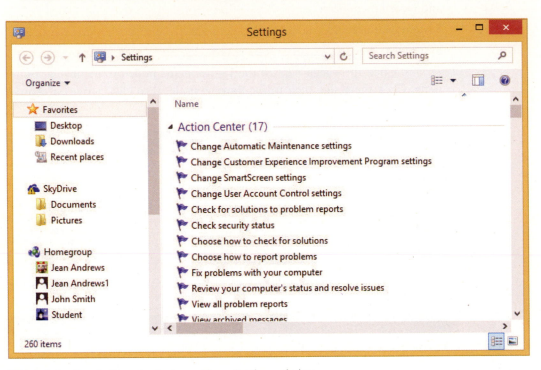

Figure C-1   The desktop shortcut provides a Settings window
Used with permission from Microsoft Corporation

REVIEW QUESTIONS

1. What are two ways to access the System window?

   _____

   _____

2. Using the charms bar, what are the steps to set the network security to a public network?

   _____

   _____

3. Based on the system information you gathered, what component of your computer would you upgrade first? Why?

   _____

   _____

4. Why is it beneficial to keep a written record of your system's configuration?

   _____

   _____

LAB C.2 PROTECT AGAINST MALWARE

OBJECTIVES

The goal of this lab is to verify your computer is clean of malicious programs using Windows Defender or using free malware removal software. After completing this lab, you will be able to:

▲ Make sure Windows Defender is turned on

▲ Check for and install the latest Windows Defender updates

▲ Scan for spyware or other malicious software infecting your computer

MATERIALS REQUIRED

This lab requires the following:

▲ Windows 8 operating system

▲ Internet access

LAB PREPARATION

Before the lab begins, the instructor or lab assistant needs to do the following:

▲ Verify that Windows starts with no errors

▲ Verify that Internet access is available

▲ Perform a backup of important files if necessary

ACTIVITY BACKGROUND

Malware removal software is one of the largest growing technology sectors today, as new malicious programs continually flood the Internet. Malware removal software is useful because malware hides from the user and is difficult to detect. As a user surfs the Web, malware can be downloaded and installed without the user's knowledge or consent.

Microsoft Windows offers Windows Defender to protect a system against spyware, viruses, and other malware. Once you turn on Windows Defender, it will run automatically to scan for malware or other unwanted programs. Definitions need to be updated daily to keep up with new malware.

ESTIMATED COMPLETION TIME: 15 Minutes

Activity

Windows Defender will not run if other antivirus software is running on your system. Follow these steps to turn off other antivirus software and then explore how Windows Defender works:

1. To find out if antivirus software is running other than Windows Defender, go to the **Windows desktop,** click the Action Center flag in the taskbar, then click **Open Action Center.** The Action Center opens.

2. Click the **Security** title to expand the Security section. If you find in the Security section that antivirus software other than Windows Defender is running, turn off this antivirus program. Close the Action Center.

C

3. To open the Windows Defender window, go to the **Start** screen, and type **defender**. Click the **Windows Defender** tile. The Windows Defender window opens (see Figure C-2). In the figure, Windows Defender shows the computer is potentially unprotected.

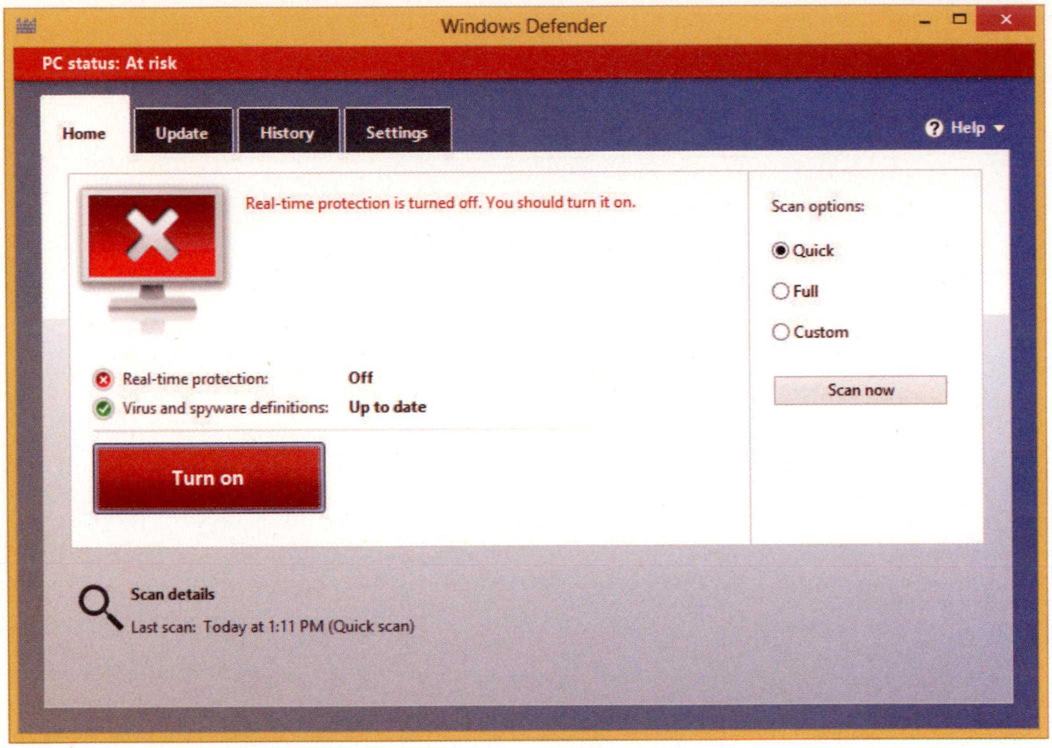

Figure C-2   Windows Defender alerts that this PC is at risk
Used with permission from Microsoft Corporation

4. If your Real-time protection is off, click the **Turn on** button.

5. Click the **Update** tab. Click **Update** to update your definitions.

After the virus and spyware definitions have finished updating, you are able to scan your computer with the most recent defenses against malware that Windows Defender offers. To scan your computer, follow these steps:

1. Return to the **Home** tab. With **Quick** selected as the scan option in the right pane, click the **Scan now** button.

2. After the scan is completed, you can see results from the scan. If any malicious software is found, complete the action requested by Windows Defender to remove the threat.

3. Repeat the scan, and remove any newly detected threats.

4. Keep repeating the scan until no threats are detected.

To change scan settings and delete quarantined items, follow these steps:

1. To change the scan settings, click the **Settings** tab. Explore the different setting groups in the left pane. After exploring, click the **Advanced** group.

2. Select the boxes you want Windows Defender to use in future scans. If you made any changes, click the **Save changes** button.

3. To remove quarantined items from your computer, click the **History** tab. If necessary, with **Quarantined items** selected, click the **View details** button.

4. Select the items to delete, and click **Remove**, or to delete all quarantined items, click **Remove all**.

REVIEW QUESTIONS

1. Why is it important to use a malware removal program, such as Windows Defender, rather than just being careful while surfing the Web?

   _____

   _____

   _____

2. Why is it important to update virus and spyware definitions on malware removal programs, and how often should they be updated?

   _____

   _____

3. Why would you want to quarantine malware, and how do you delete the malware from your system? Why could this be important?

   _____

   _____

   _____

   _____

4. What are the options available in the Windows Defender settings? Why is the Real-Time Protection option important?

   _____

   _____

   _____

   _____

   _____

LAB C.3 USE THE PROBLEM STEPS RECORDER

OBJECTIVES

The goal of this lab is to help you use the Windows 8 Steps Recorder. After completing this lab, you will be able to:

◢ Record steps using Steps Recorder

◢ Review steps recorded

C

MATERIALS REQUIRED

This lab requires the following:

▲ Windows 8 operating system

LAB PREPARATION

Before the lab begins, the instructor or lab assistant needs to do the following:

▲ Verify that Windows 8 starts with no errors

ACTIVITY BACKGROUND

When you're troubleshooting a problem in Windows, recording the steps you take can be crucial to proper documentation. Recording steps is also helpful when you're documenting how to do something or a user needs to show you what he or she is doing. Fortunately, Microsoft provides Steps Recorder to record steps and generate a report with all actions recorded.

ESTIMATED COMPLETION TIME: 20 Minutes

Activity

Follow these steps to use Steps Recorder:

1. On the Start screen, start typing **Steps Recorder**. Click the **Steps Recorder** tile. The Steps Recorder program opens on the desktop.

2. Click **Start Record**. The Steps Recorder begins recording all actions on the computer.

3. Return to the **Start** screen, and type **paint**. Click the **Paint** tile. The Paint program opens on the desktop. Note that when you click, a red dot appears. This indicates that this action was recorded.

4. Draw a mark or shape on the paint window.

5. Click **Stop Record** in the Steps Recorder program. The Steps Recorder automatically opens a file containing all the steps and information that was recorded. Scroll down the window to review the images and scripted steps of your actions recorded while opening the Paint program and drawing an image in the Paint window. See Figure C-3.

6. In the Steps Recorder window showing the file containing the steps, click **Save**.

7. Save this report to your computer, and name it **UsingPaint.zip**. Close the Steps Recorder and Paint windows (no need to save changes in Paint).

8. Open the UsingPaint.zip compressed folder, and open the recording file. Review your recording, and close the file.

REVIEW QUESTIONS

1. How do you know an action using the mouse is recorded?

   _____

2. What type of folder contains the file of recorded steps?

   _____

3. What type of file contains the recorded steps? By default, which program is used to view the file?

   _____

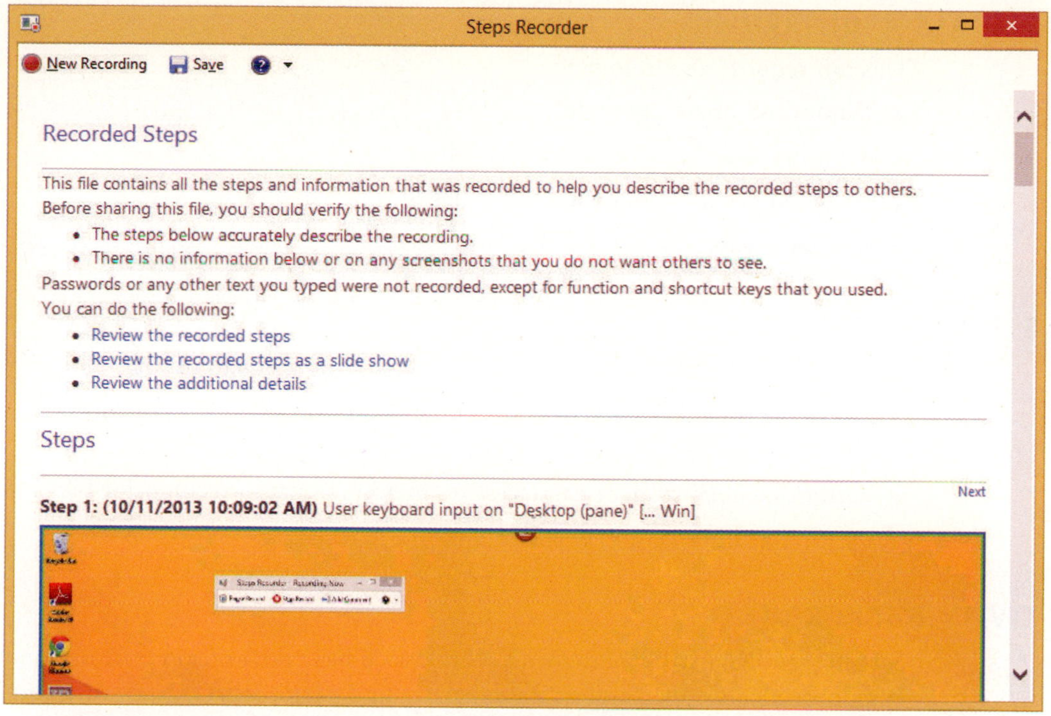

Figure C-3 The Steps Recorder records screen captures and detailed steps of user activity
Used with permission from Microsoft Corporation

4. Does Steps Recorder record a script of the actions taken or images of the actions taken?

_____

5. Imagine you have a job working on a help desk. What is a possible situation when you might use the Steps Recorder?

_____

_____

_____

LAB C.4 EXPLORE TOOLS TO SOLVE WINDOWS 8 STARTUP PROBLEMS

OBJECTIVES

The goal of this lab is to have you explore tools to solve Windows 8 startup problems. After completing this lab, you will be able to:

▲ Find troubleshooting tools for Windows startup problems

▲ Use the Startup Repair process

▲ Enable and disable the Advanced Boot Options menu

▲ Boot to Safe Mode with Networking

C

MATERIALS REQUIRED

This lab requires the following:

- ◢ Windows 8 operating system
- ◢ Windows 8 setup DVD or recovery drive
- ◢ An account with administrator privileges
- ◢ Internet access

LAB PREPARATION

Before the lab begins, the instructor or lab assistant needs to do the following:

- ◢ Verify that Windows starts with no errors and the Windows 8 setup DVD or a recovery drive is available
- ◢ Verify that each student has access to an administrator account for his or her system
- ◢ Verify that Internet access is available

ACTIVITY BACKGROUND

Startup problems can be annoying. Windows 8 has taken great effort to minimize this pain. Windows 8 is one of the most stable operating systems with the fewest errors at startup. On the third sequential reboot, Windows 8 automatically starts a self-healing process. After Windows 8 has attempted to heal itself and you still encounter a hang up, error message, stop error, or hardware error, you can use the startup repair tools in this lab to help you resolve startup problems.

ESTIMATED COMPLETION TIME: 45 minutes

Activity

This lab is divided into two parts. In the first part, you use the charms bar to explore several Windows 8 tools used to fix startup problems. You also use the Startup Repair tool and boot into Safe Mode with Networking. In the second part of the lab, you enable the Advanced Boot Options menu and boot into Safe Mode with Networking. As you work through this lab, reference Figure C-4 to keep track of where you find each of the startup troubleshooting tools.

Part 1: Find tools to fix startup problems

Follow these steps to locate startup repair tools:

1. Sign in to your system with an administrator account.
2. On the **charms bar**, select the **Settings** charm. Click **Change PC settings**.
3. On the PC settings page, click **Update and recovery** in the left pane.
4. On the Update and recovery page, click **Recovery** in the left pane. List the options for recovering your PC that can be accessed through the Settings charm and briefly describe the purpose of each one:

_____

_____

_____

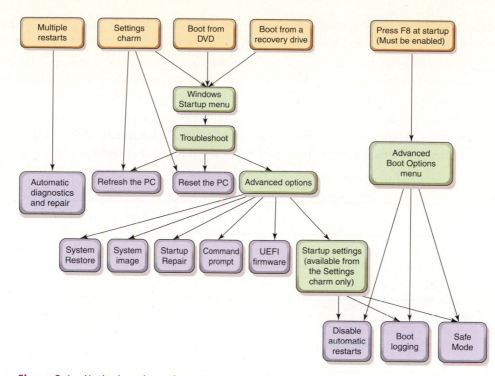

Figure C-4 Methods to boot the system, menus that appear, and tools available on menus used to troubleshoot startup problems
Copyright © 2015 Cengage Learning

5. Click **Restart now** under the Advanced startup option. Your computer restarts. When given an option, select **Troubleshoot**, then **Advanced options**. Under Advanced options, list the tools available to troubleshoot startup problems and briefly describe the purpose of each:

   _____

   _____

   _____

   _____

   _____

   _____

6. Select **Startup Repair**. Your computer restarts into Startup Repair.

7. Choose your account name. Enter your password. Click **Continue**.

8. Startup Repair diagnoses your system and reports its findings. Click **Advanced options**. This returns you to the Windows Startup menu.

9. Click **Troubleshoot**, then **Advanced options**.

10. Click **Startup Settings**. Click **Restart**.

11. Listed are options for changing startup behavior. Press **5** or **F5** on your keyboard to select **Enable Safe Mode with Networking**. The system reboots. After you sign in, Safe Mode with Networking loads.

12. Open **Internet Explorer**, and make sure the Internet is available.

13. Use the **Settings** charm to **Restart** the system.

C

If the hard drive is so corrupted you cannot boot to it, you must boot from another bootable media. Follow these steps to explore the troubleshooting tools available when booting from other bootable media:

1. Boot from the Windows setup DVD or a recovery drive, and select your language and keyboard layout. (Know that before you can boot to media other than the hard drive, you might need to first change the boot priority order in BIOS setup.)

2. When the Windows Setup screen appears, click **Repair your computer**. On the next screen, select your keyboard layout. Next select the correct troubleshooting options on each screen that appears until you reach the Advanced options screen.

   ◢ Under Advanced options, list the tools available:

   _____

   _____

   _____

   _____

   ◢ Which tool is not available on this screen that was available in Step 5 above when you used the Settings charm to restart the system?

   _____

3. Launch Windows 8 normally, and remove the bootable media from your computer.

Part 2: Enable and use the Advanced Boot Options menu

Safe Mode can be extremely useful when you're trying to solve a problem with a corrupted device driver or with a malware infection because the driver or malware may not load when Safe Mode is launched. By default in Windows 8, Safe Mode is launched only from the Settings charm. If you cannot start Windows properly, you cannot use the Settings charm to access Safe Mode.

> 📝 **Notes** This part of the lab will not work if your computer is set for dual boot.

Another way to launch Safe Mode is to press F8 at startup to launch the Advanced Boot Options menu. By default, this option is disabled. To use F8 at startup, you must enable it before you encounter a startup problem. Follow these steps to enable the use of F8 during startup:

1. On the Start screen, type **command**. Right-click the **Command Prompt** tile that appears, and select **Run as administrator** in the status bar. Respond to the UAC box. The command prompt window opens on the desktop with administrative privileges.

2. In the command prompt window enter this command:
   bcdedit /set {default} bootmenupolicy legacy
   Press **Enter**.

3. Restart your system. When Windows first starts to load, press **F8** to access the Advanced Boot Options menu. List the options available to change the boot behavior:

   _____

   _____

   _____

   _____

_____

_____

4. Select **Safe Mode with Networking,** and press **Enter.** The system reboots. After you sign in, Safe Mode with Networking loads.

5. Use the Settings charm to **Restart** the system.

If your instructor asks you to disable the use of F8 at startup, follow these steps to disable the F8 option:

1. Open a command prompt window with administrative privileges.

2. In the command prompt window, enter this command:
   bcdedit /set {default} bootmenupolicy standard
   Press **Enter.**

3. Close all open windows.

REVIEW QUESTIONS

1. Why is Windows 8 considered to be a more stable system than previous Windows editions regarding startup problems?

_____

_____

2. Using the charms bar, list the steps you take to find the Refresh the PC option.

_____

_____

_____

_____

3. What is the difference between a refresh and a reset?

_____

_____

_____

4. Why would you want the F8 option at startup enabled on a system?

_____

_____

5. What is the command line you enter into the command prompt window to disable the F8 option at startup?

_____

6. If the hard drive is so corrupted that pressing F8 at startup cannot load the Advanced Boot Options menu, how should you boot the system so you can attempt to repair the Windows installation?

_____

C

LAB C.5 CREATE AND USE A CUSTOM REFRESH IMAGE

OBJECTIVES

The goal of this lab is to help you create and use a custom refresh image. After completing this lab, you will be able to:

▲ Create a custom refresh image

▲ Refresh your system using your custom refresh image

MATERIALS REQUIRED

This lab requires the following:

▲ Windows 8 operating system

▲ Internet access

▲ Account with administrative privileges

LAB PREPARATION

Before the lab begins, the instructor or lab assistant needs to do the following:

▲ Verify that Windows 8 starts with no errors

▲ Verify that Internet access is available

▲ Verify that each student has an administrator account for his or her system

ACTIVITY BACKGROUND

If your system isn't running well, you might want to refresh or reset it. A refresh is preferred to a reset because a refresh retains user settings, data, and Windows 8 apps. A refresh works even better if you have created a custom refresh image to use during the refresh. Using the image, the system is restored to the point it was when the image was created, and then any user settings, data, or Windows 8 apps that were installed or changed since the image was created are also restored to the system. After you refresh your system using a custom refresh image, you will need to reinstall any desktop applications that were not installed at the time you created the custom refresh image.

Best practice is to create a custom refresh image after you have the system configured just the way you want it. A custom refresh image takes a snapshot or image of the current system and stores in the image the Windows installation, all installed applications, and user settings and data.

In this lab, you make some changes to user settings, data files, and installed apps. Next you create a custom refresh image, and then make additional changes to user settings, data files, and installed apps. Next, you refresh the system, and then examine the system to find out which changes are retained by the refresh. By working your way through this lab, you can be confident you understand exactly how a refresh works and what to expect from one.

ESTIMATED COMPLETION TIME: 60–120 Minutes

Activity

Follow these steps to customize your computer:

1. Sign in using an administrator account.

2. From the Start screen, on the **charms bar**, click the **Settings** charm. Click **Personalize**. Select a picture for the Start screen background, and select a **Background color**. Describe the picture and color you selected:

3. Visit **www.google.com/chrome**, and download and install the free web browser, Google Chrome.

4. Create a new document, and save it in your Documents folder. What is the file name and path to your document?

_____

Follow these steps to create a custom refresh image:

1. On the Start screen, move your pointer to the bottom of the screen, and click the **down arrow**. On the Apps screen, scroll to the right, and under the *Windows System* section, find the Command Prompt tile. Right-click **Command Prompt**. In the status bar, click **Run as administrator**. Respond to the UAC box. The command prompt window opens.

2. Enter this command, substituting any drive and folder for that shown in the command line:
   recimg /createimage C:\MyImage

3. The image is created and registered. In the command prompt, enter this command:
   recimg /showcurrent

4. The location of the image is displayed. Write down the location of the image.

_____

5. Close the command prompt window. Open File Explorer, and browse to the image file. What is the location given in your address bar? What is the size of the image file?

_____

_____

Follow these steps to make additional changes to your system:

1. From the Start screen, open the **Settings** charm, and click **Personalize**. Select a picture for the Start screen background and a background color different from those you selected at the beginning of this lab. Describe the new picture and color you selected:

_____

2. Go to **mozilla-firefox.todownload.com**, and download and install the Mozilla Firefox browser.

3. Open the Store app, and install a Windows 8 app. Which application did you install?

_____

4. Delete the file you stored in your Documents folder earlier in the lab.

Follow these steps to refresh the system using the custom refresh image you created earlier:

1. On the **charms bar**, select the **Settings** charm. Click **Change PC settings**.

2. On the PC settings page, click **Update and recovery** in the left pane.

3. On the Update and recovery page, click **Recovery** in the left pane.

4. Under Refresh your PC without affecting your files, click **Get started**.

5. On the Refresh your PC screen, review what will happen when you perform a refresh. Click **Next**.

6. Click **Refresh**. During the refresh process, your system restarts.

Do the following to find out the results of the refresh:

1. Sign on to your system and answer the following questions:

   ◢ Does the Start screen use the latest picture and background color you selected? Why or why not?

_____

◢ Is the app you installed from the Windows Store still installed? Why or why not?

_____

◢ Is the file you stored in your Documents folder there? Why or why not?

_____

◢ Is Google Chrome installed as a desktop app? Why or why not?

_____

◢ Is Mozilla Firefox installed as a desktop app? Why or why not?

_____

2. Browse to the root of drive C. What is the size of the Windows.old folder?

_____

3. Open the file stored on the Windows desktop that lists the desktop applications that were removed from your computer during the refresh. Which application(s) were removed during the refresh?

_____

Now it's time to clean up the system. Do the following:

1. To keep your hard drive clean, it's best to delete the Windows.old folder after you have confirmed that the refresh was successful. Delete the **Windows.old** folder.

2. Uninstall any Windows 8 apps or desktop applications that you installed in this lab that are still installed.

3. If your instructor requests it, delete the custom refresh image you created in this lab.

REVIEW QUESTIONS

1. What command line can you enter into the command prompt window to view the location of the active recovery image?

_____

2. What is the file name of the refresh image?

_____

3. When you perform a system refresh, how will your PC settings be changed?

_____

4. When you perform a system refresh without the help of a custom refresh image, some apps are kept and some are removed. Which apps are kept? Which are removed? How do you know which apps will be removed?

_____

_____

_____

LAB C.6: SABOTAGE AND REPAIR WINDOWS 8

OBJECTIVES

The goal of this lab is to learn to troubleshoot Windows 8 by repairing a sabotaged system. After completing this lab, you will be able to:

◢ Troubleshoot and repair a system that isn't working correctly

MATERIALS REQUIRED

This lab requires the following:

◢ Windows 8 installed on a PC designated for sabotage

◢ Windows 8 setup DVD or installation files

◢ A workgroup of 2 to 4 students

> 📝 **Notes** This lab works great on Windows 8 installed in a VM.

LAB PREPARATION

Before the lab begins, the instructor or lab assistant needs to do the following:

◢ Verify that Windows starts with no errors

◢ Provide each workgroup with access to the Windows 8 installation files, if needed

ACTIVITY BACKGROUND

You have learned about several tools and methods you can use to recover Windows 8 when it fails. This lab gives you the opportunity to use these skills in a troubleshooting situation. Your group will sabotage another group's system while that group sabotages your system. Then your group will repair its own system.

ESTIMATED COMPLETION TIME: 45 Minutes

🖳 **Activity**

1. If your system's hard drive contains important data, back it up to another medium. Is there anything else you would like to back up before another group sabotages the system? Record the name and location of that item here, and then back it up:

   _____

2. Trade systems with another group, and sabotage the other group's system while they sabotage your system. Do one thing that will cause the system to fail to boot, display errors after the boot, or prevent a device or application from working. The following list offers some sabotage suggestions. Do something in the following list, or think of another option. (Do not alter the hardware.)

   ◢ Find a system file in the root directory that's required to boot the computer, and rename it or move it to a different directory. (Don't delete the file.)

   ◢ Using the Registry Editor (Regedit.exe), delete several important keys or values in the Registry.

◢ Locate important system files in the \Windows folder or its subfolders, and rename them or move them to another directory.

> **Notes** To move, delete, or rename a Windows system file, you might need to first take ownership of the file and gain full access to it using the **takeown** and **icacls** commands. The Microsoft Knowledge Base Article 929833 at support.microsoft.com explains how to use these two commands in Windows 7/ Vista, which also work in Windows 8.

◢ Put a corrupted program file in the folder that will cause the program to launch automatically at startup. Record the name of that program file and folder here:

_____

◢ Use display settings that aren't readable, such as black text on a black background.

◢ Disable a critical device driver or Windows service.

3. Reboot the system, and verify that a problem exists.

4. How did you sabotage the other team's system?

_____

_____

5. Return to your system, and troubleshoot it.

6. Describe the problem as a user would describe it to you if you were working at a help desk:

_____

_____

_____

7. What is your first guess as to the source of the problem?

_____

8. An expert problem solver always tries the simple things first. What is an easy fix that you can try? Try the fix, and record the results.

_____

_____

9. As you troubleshoot the system, list the high-level steps you are taking in the troubleshooting process and explain beside each step why you decided to take that step:

_____

_____

_____

_____

10. How did you finally solve the problem and return the system to good working order?

_____

_____

REVIEW QUESTIONS

1. What would you do differently the next time you encountered the same symptoms that you encountered in this lab?

_____

_____

2. What Windows utilities did you use or could you have used to solve the problem in the lab?

_____

3. What might cause the problem in the lab to occur in real life? List three possible causes:

_____

_____

_____

4. If you were the PC support technician responsible for this computer in an office environment, what could you do to prevent this problem from happening in the future or limit its impact on users if it did happen?

_____

_____

C

INDEX